FRANCO IS DEAD! ¡VIVA ESPAÑA!

A MEMOIR IN POEMS AND PHOTOGRAPHS

Barbara Strelke

Franco Is Dead! ¡Viva España!: A Memoir in Poems and Photographs

Published by Studio 218 Press
Email: studio218press@gmail.com
barbarastrelke.com

ISBN: 978-0-692-09863-9
LCCN: 2018903826

Contents

A Place Captured in Time

Franco is Dead! ¡Viva España! is a photographic and poetic memoir of Spain in the late 1970s. The photographs and poems were originally part of my longer memoir, *Journey Home Times Four.* But *Franco is Dead! ¡Viva España!* didn't quite fit my original home-place concept which focused on my four long-term homes in Central Wisconsin, New Mexico, Tucson, Arizona, and San Carlos, Mexico.

I had lived in Spain for an extended period of time 40 years ago, and visited nearly a dozen times since then, but I was always a foreigner, at best an ex-pat, often a tourist. It never became "home" with the complications, ambiguities, and duties you feel toward "home." Although I love the landscape of Iberia, know its history better than that of my own country, and treasure the generosity and hardiness of its people, I'm still a visitor and outsider. It is a place and a people I can say I love, but it's the carefree love of kinship once or twice removed: the love of a grandparent for her grandchild. I can spoil him and see only his talents and charm, and leave his home before I run out of energy or outstay my welcome.

Did I fall in love with Spain because the landscape reminded me of New Mexico, my first home as an adult? Spain seemed familiar and comforting. When I first visited in the summer of 1977, I was in the company of friends from Santa Fe. My friends were John "Jack" Masters and his wife Barbara who had invited me to be part of their "walking" group. I would learn later that "walking" was British English for strenuous trekking.

Jack and Barbara had been walking in the mountains of northern Spain for 20 years, exploring both the *Picos de Europa*, the limestone range in northern Spain located south of the Bay of Biscay, and the Pyrenees, the mountain range that forms the northeastern border between Spain and France. The Masters had lived in Santa Fe for most of the year and hiked in the *Sangre de Cristos*. That's where I had met them, when for a brief time I hiked with the Santa Fe Chile and Marching Society, a group that was Jack's brain child. But for two or three months each summer, with friends from New Mexico in tow, they moved their operational headquarters (think military tactical planning) to Spain. Jack was a best-selling novelist (*Bhowani Junction; The Deceivers, Nightrunners of Bengal,* among others) and retired British officer in the Indian Army. After Indian independence, they had moved to the United States, first to Rockland County, near New York City, then to Santa Fe.

Life is a miracle of chance occurrences, and meeting Jack was one of those miracles. I was barely 30 and although not a stranger to literature or travel—I already had a couple of degrees in English literature and had hitchhiked in Europe, I was young and impressionable. Jack's humor, generous spirit, and exotic personal history captivated me. He was a natural story-teller, with a rugged and weathered face that lit up when he was telling a story or a ribald joke. One of his passions was hiking, and it seemed to share a symbiotic relationship with writing. Long hikes, even with a troop of followers, gave Jack time to tune out and think about his story lines, plotting, and character development. Once he told me he could work out his problems with writing—a rough passage or problem transition, while he was pacing up the mountain, as long as he knew everyone was safe and the trail was familiar. He was a quiet and solitary hiker, lost in his thoughts, followed by his wife with her characteristic hand on hip and other hand on her walking stick. The rest of the more chatty members of the marching society followed a respectful few paces behind.

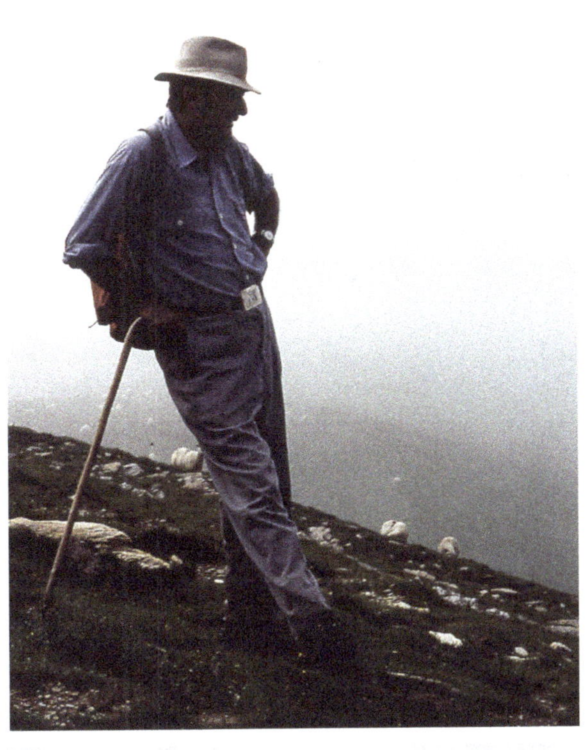

Jack Masters above Super Espot, Pyrenees

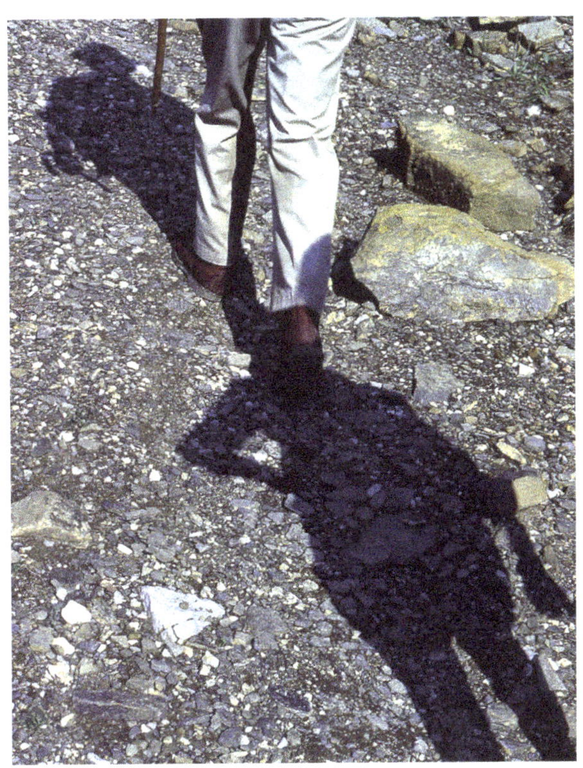

Shadows of Jack and Barbara Masters

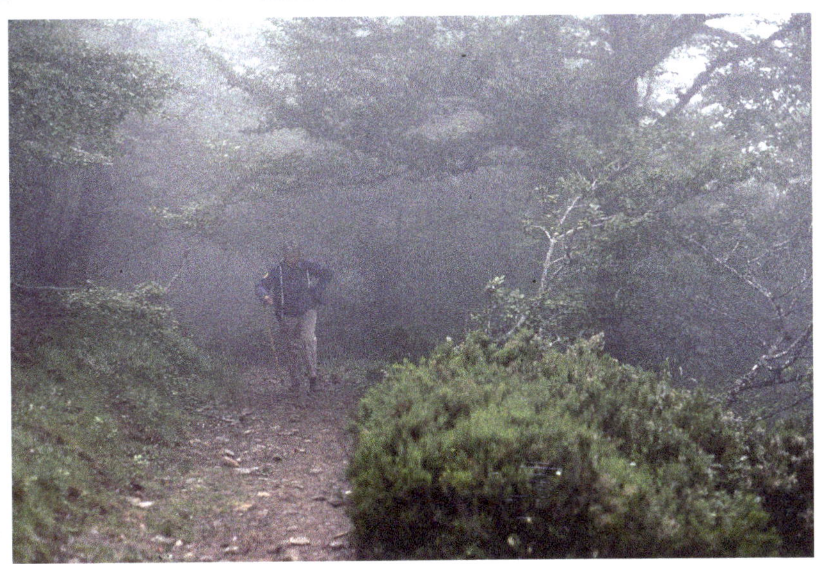

Barbara Masters, *Picos de Europa*

I recall, that to help with my expenses for the Spanish trip, Jack gave me his old IBM Selectric that I sold for $350 dollars. Probably at that time it was half my round trip flight to Spain. I made my travel arrangements in January but in February I married the man I had been with for several years. Since the trip was planned before my marriage, I didn't change my travel plans. My new husband, Don, a professor of mathematics at the University of New Mexico, was invited to join our walking group, but he said he would teach summer school and help pay for my trip.

It wasn't as if I couldn't pay my own way. I had been working for the New Mexico Commission on Aging as a public information specialist. When I knew my vacation was to be Spain, I decided to make it a working vacation. I requested an additional two weeks off on administrative leave because I proposed doing a photo-essay on "*Los Ancianos de España.*" My boss, the former Lieutenant Governor, Roberto Mondragón, was sympathetic to my creative proposal.

So my first trip to Spain was for walking and photography. Because Jack had planned every detail of the trip like a military campaign, not only which peak to ascend, but where we would stop for our chocolate and Maria biscuit break, my only decisions were what and who to photograph and what to order for dinner. Only many years later, after I had visited some of the same places many times, and even photographed some of the same people (the "bread lady" and the "milk lady"—*los ancianos* in 1977 encountered again in 1985 and 2001) did I appreciate the comfort level that comes with knowing a place intimately. My love of maps, particularly contour maps and USGS quads, began that summer of 1977 when Jack would gather us together over our evening drinks to study our trail for the following day. Our trek up the flanks of *Aneto* and *Monte Perdido* in the Aragón Pyrenees was not the Burma campaign, which Jack wrote about in the second volume of his autobiography, *The Road Past Mandalay*. Now Jack was leading his wife and two other women on the assault, not a battalion of Gurkas. And our civilian troop had time to identify wildflowers and chat with shepherds who we met as we marched through the high meadows.

It was a glorious month of hiking, photographing, enjoying friends, and eating and drinking: nearly all the essentials of a full life, as I think about it now. We stayed in comfortable hotels so our creature needs were met. I missed Don and didn't have time for reading—two other joys of life, but it was an adventure in the rugged valleys and lush high meadows of a foreign country. We were surrounded by beauty—a backdrop of snow covered peaks, a foreground of alpine flowers, and every now and then the surprise of encountering shepherds who were resting along the trail while their sheep and goats looked like white specks against the mountain slope.

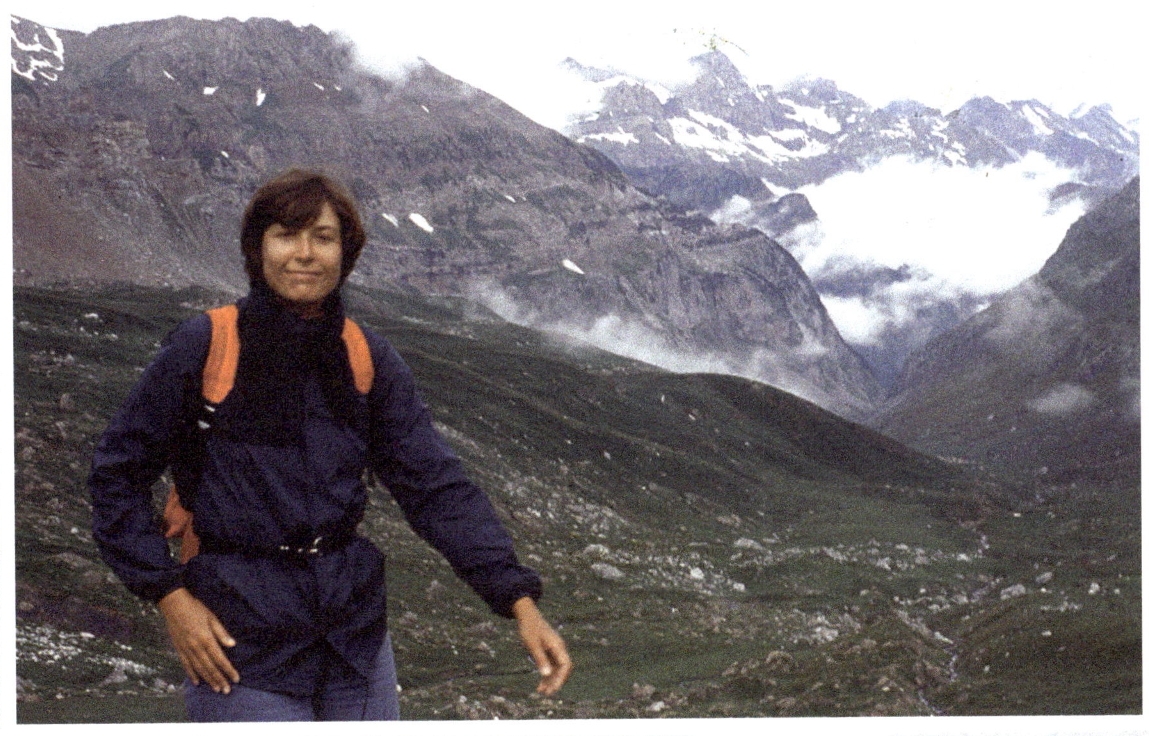

My first hike in the Pyrenees (photo by Jack Masters)

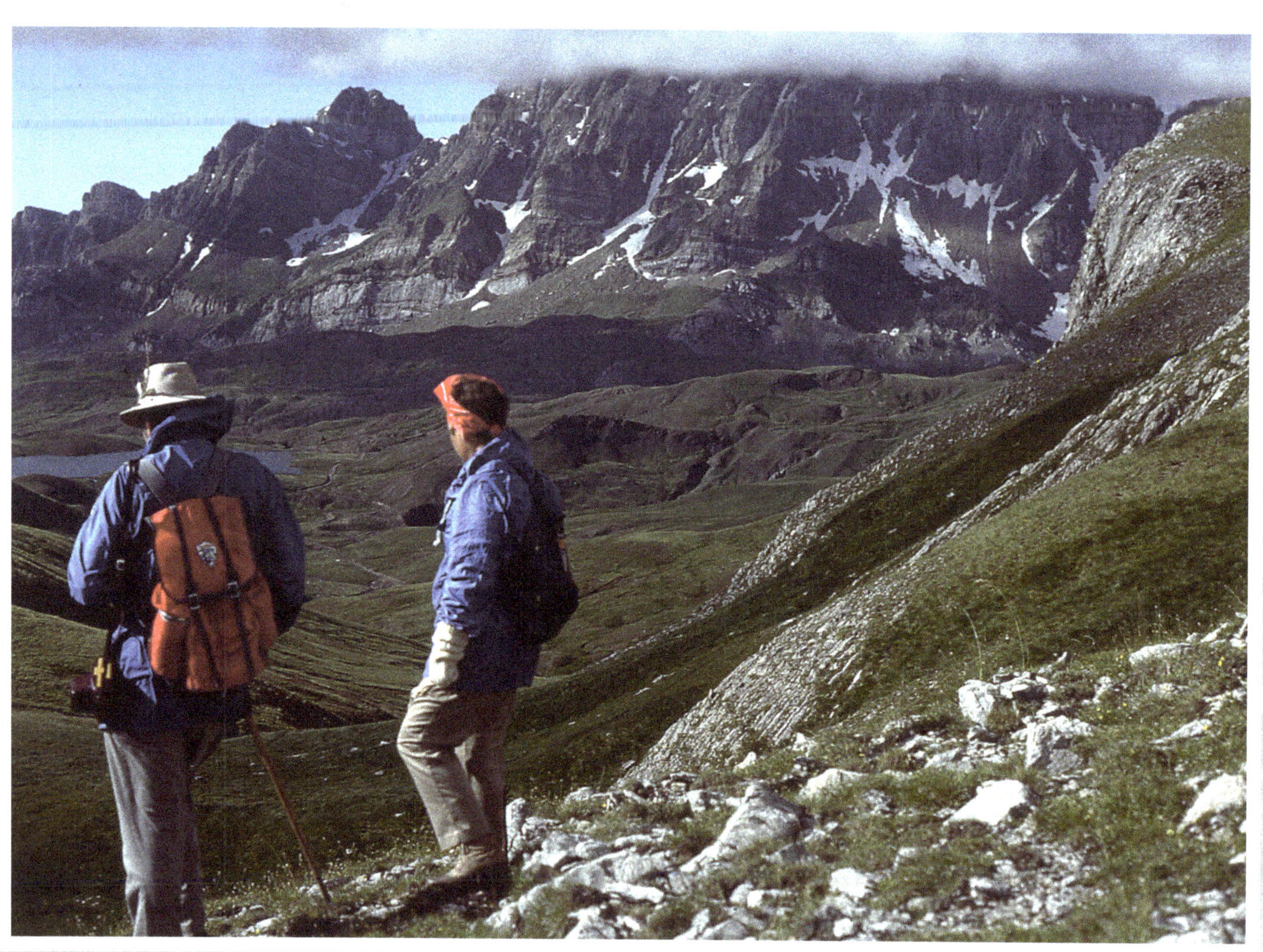

Jack and Sue, Escarra hike, Pyrenees

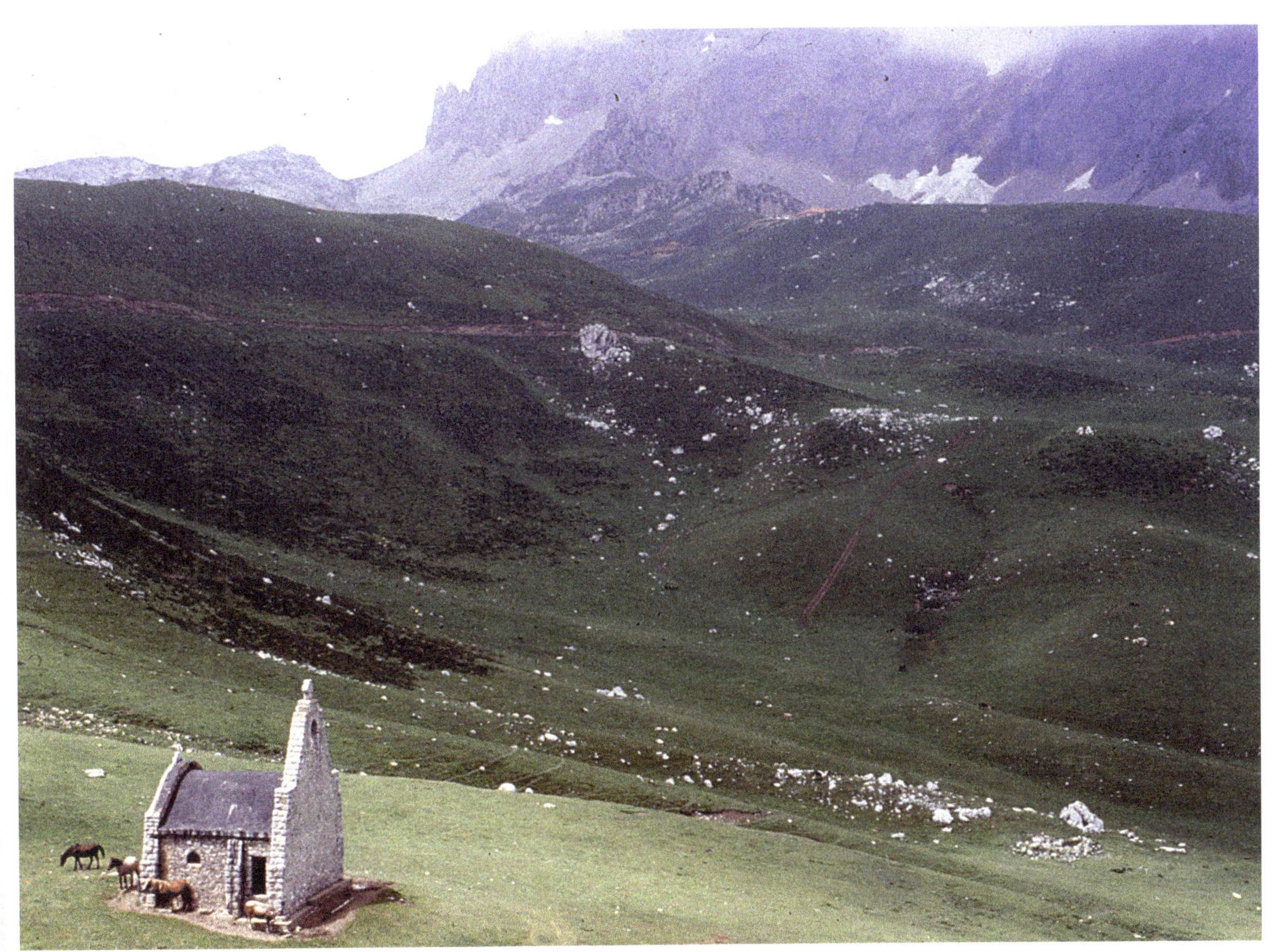

High meadow in the *Picos de Europa*

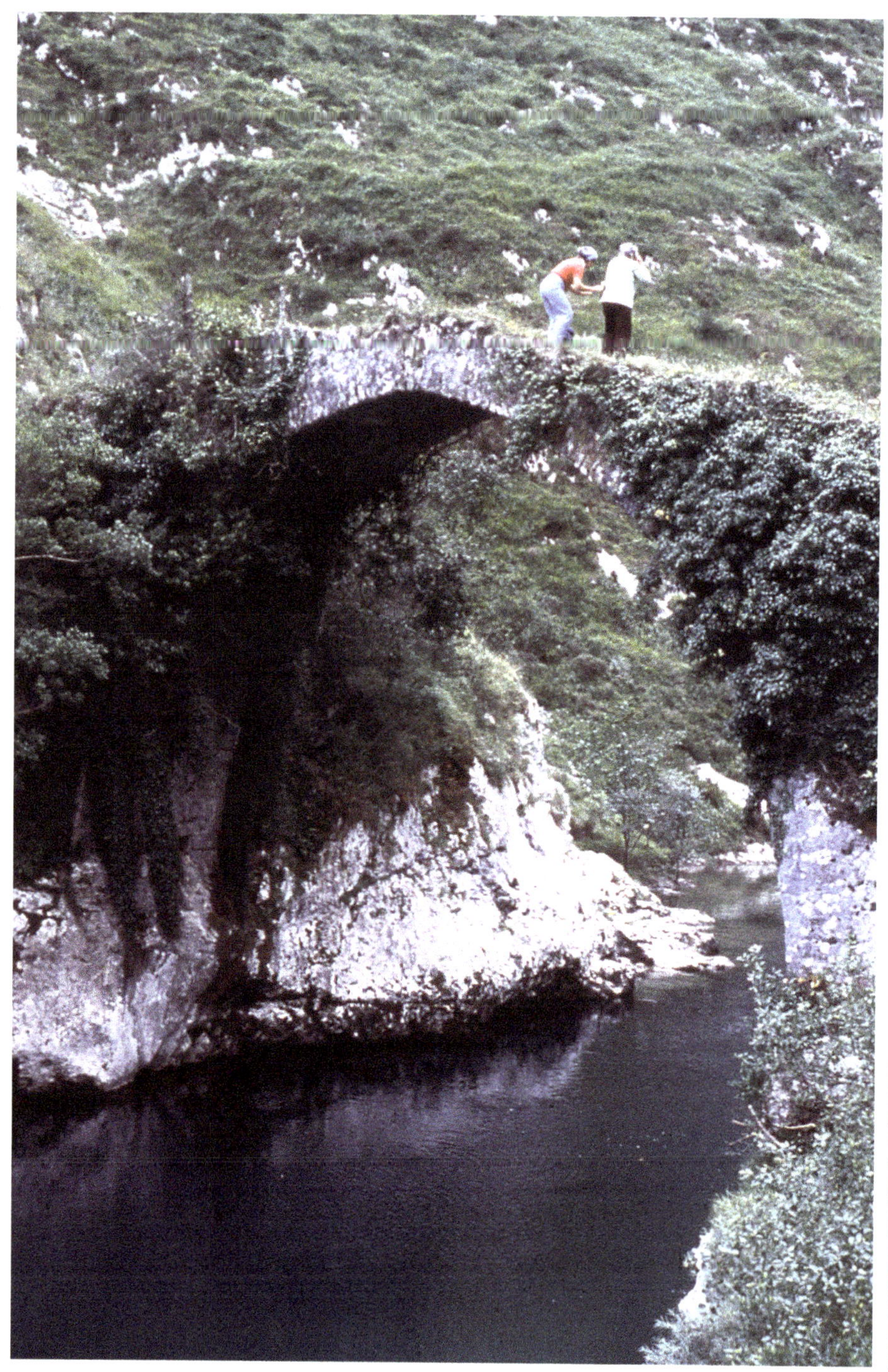

Romanesque bridge over the Río Cares, *Picos de Europa*

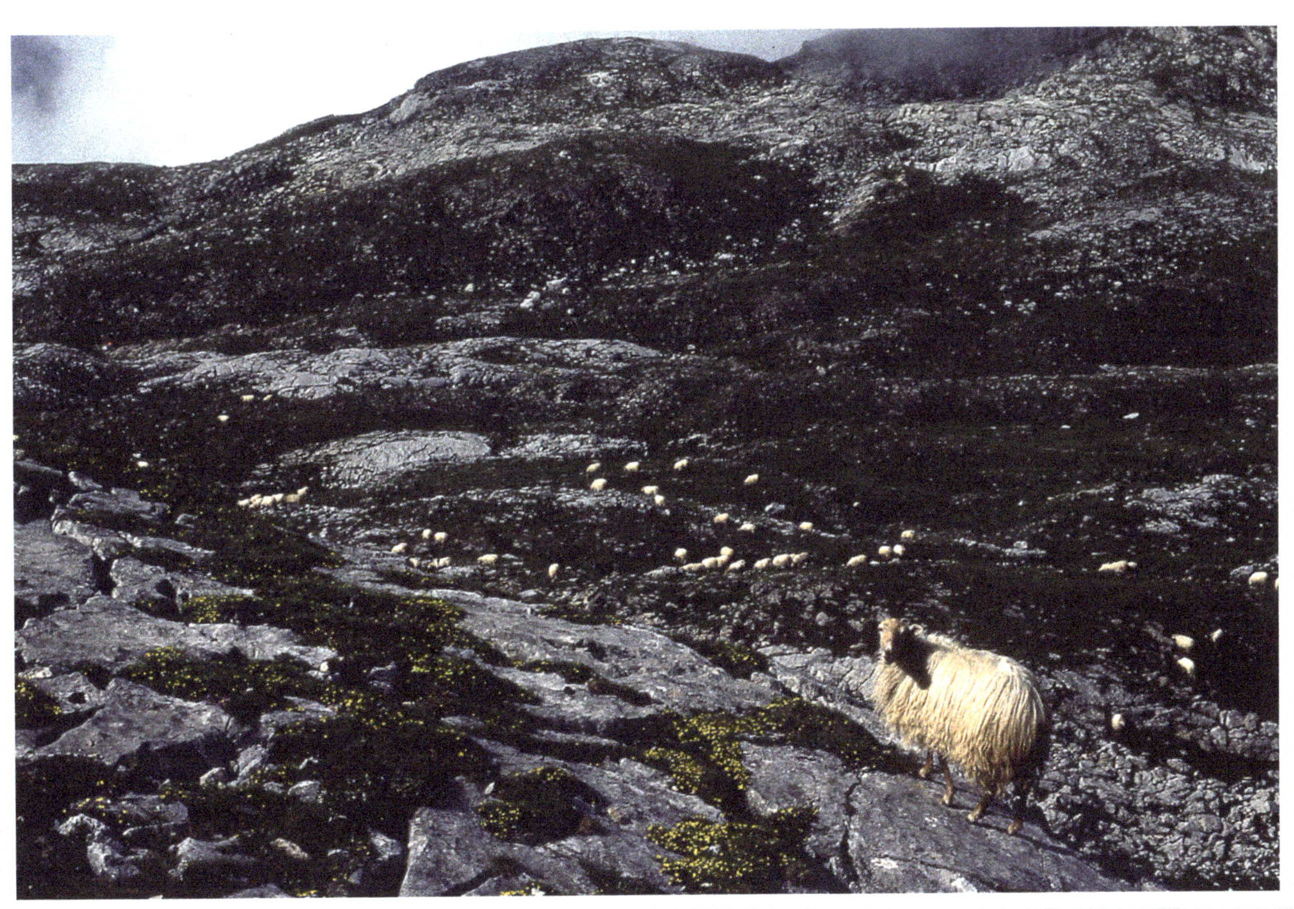

On a trail in the *Picos de Europa*

Since Jack and Barbara kept a car in Spain, they knew the roads and were friends with "road-menders" and bar owners, and had their favorite mechanics and roadside *restaurateurs*. For the years he hiked in Spain, Jack avoided the big cities, and steered clear of other writers, whether English-speaking or Spanish. We were there for the mountains and the sweet life encountered in small towns and villages. By this time, Jack and Barbara were in their sixties, but they never thought of themselves as old, nor did they think that the *ancianos* I was photographing bore any similarity to them. Our long treks often began at dawn and ended late in the afternoon at a bar where we would toast our hiking success with *anis seco* and *San Miguel* beer chasers. Our longest hike was nineteen miles, our shortest five.

In the *Picos,* in a high village of the central massif, I photographed villagers who were scything and raking their sheaves of hay and alfalfa on the steep fields near Tresviso. I practiced my elementary Spanish *("hay permiso para un foto de usted")* and gained a new appreciation of *los ancianos.* Many of the village workers were "*los ancianos*" or "*los viejos*" because so many of the younger generations had moved to the regional capitals of Santander or Bilbao, or to Madrid, or even emigrated to North or South America.

This first hike to Tresviso was a lonely journey. I had started with Barbara at the trail-head off the valley road to head up the shorter, steeper route to the village, while Jack and Sue were approaching from across a high meadow. Our plan was to meet in Tresviso, a high and isolated village in the *Picos* range. But Barbara turned back midway up the trail and I was on my own. I remember swatting flies away from my face and sweaty arms, swearing loudly, counting each step, and stopping to breathe deeply every 100 steps. Only then could I admire the scenery and regain my confidence. The day was nearly cloudless and from my ascending perch I could look back at the progress I had made and make a photographic record of the thread of switchbacks. I knew it was only six miles or so but the 4,000+ feet elevation gain made this hike a challenge.

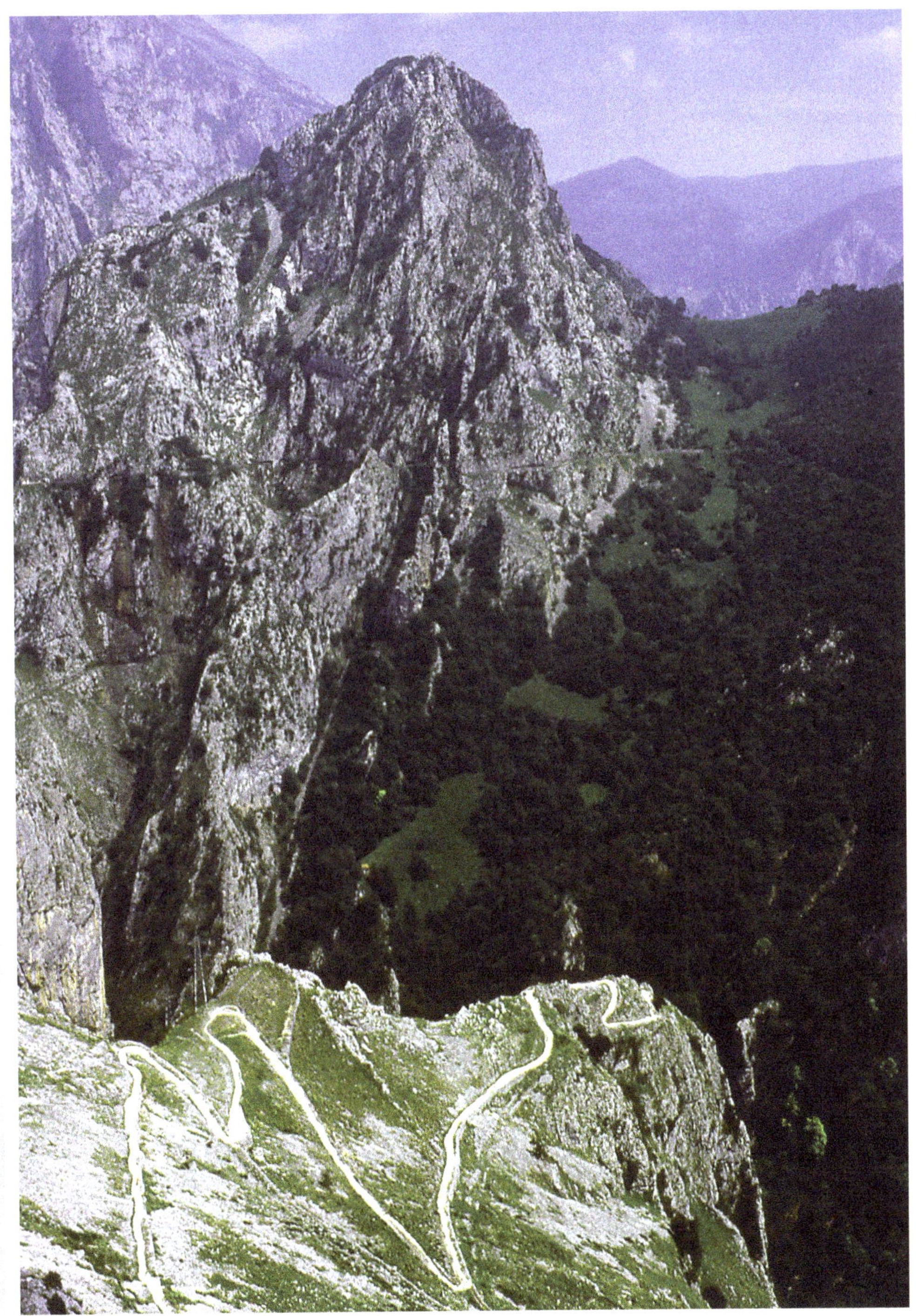

Switchback trail to Tresviso, *Picos de Europa*, Cantabria

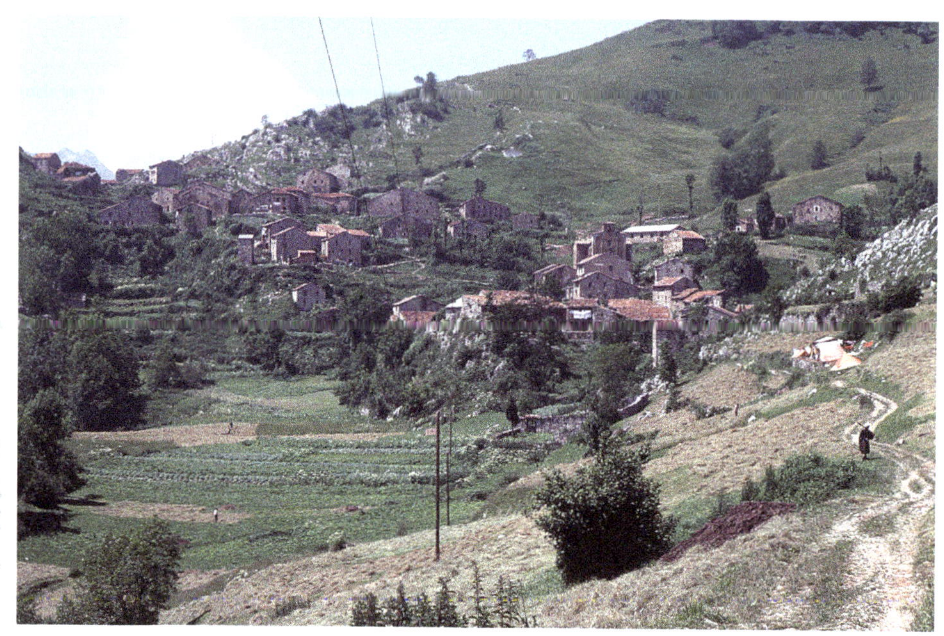

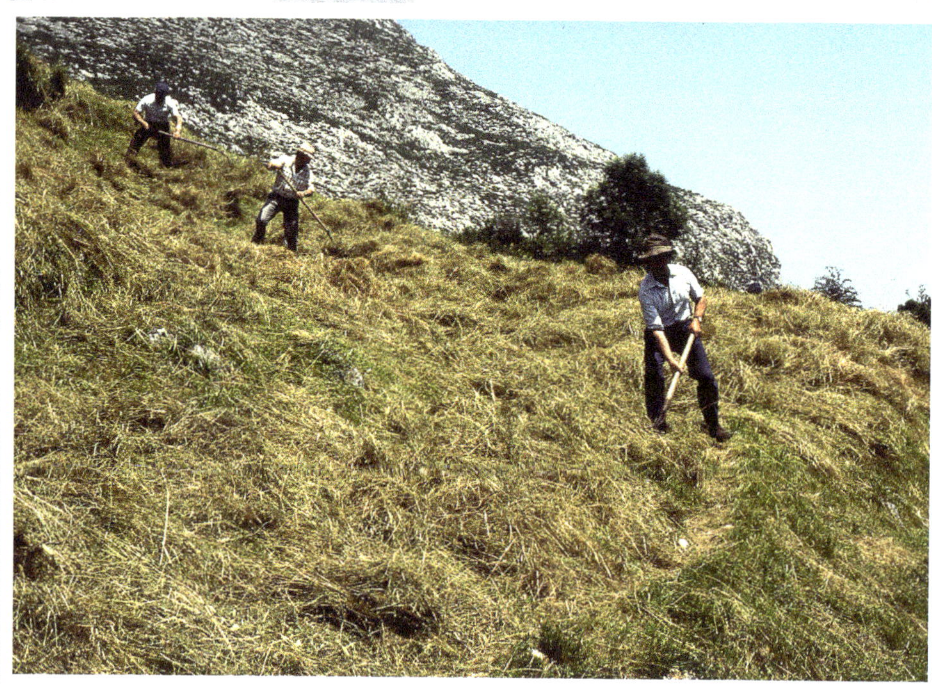

Tresviso village scenes, pages 12-15

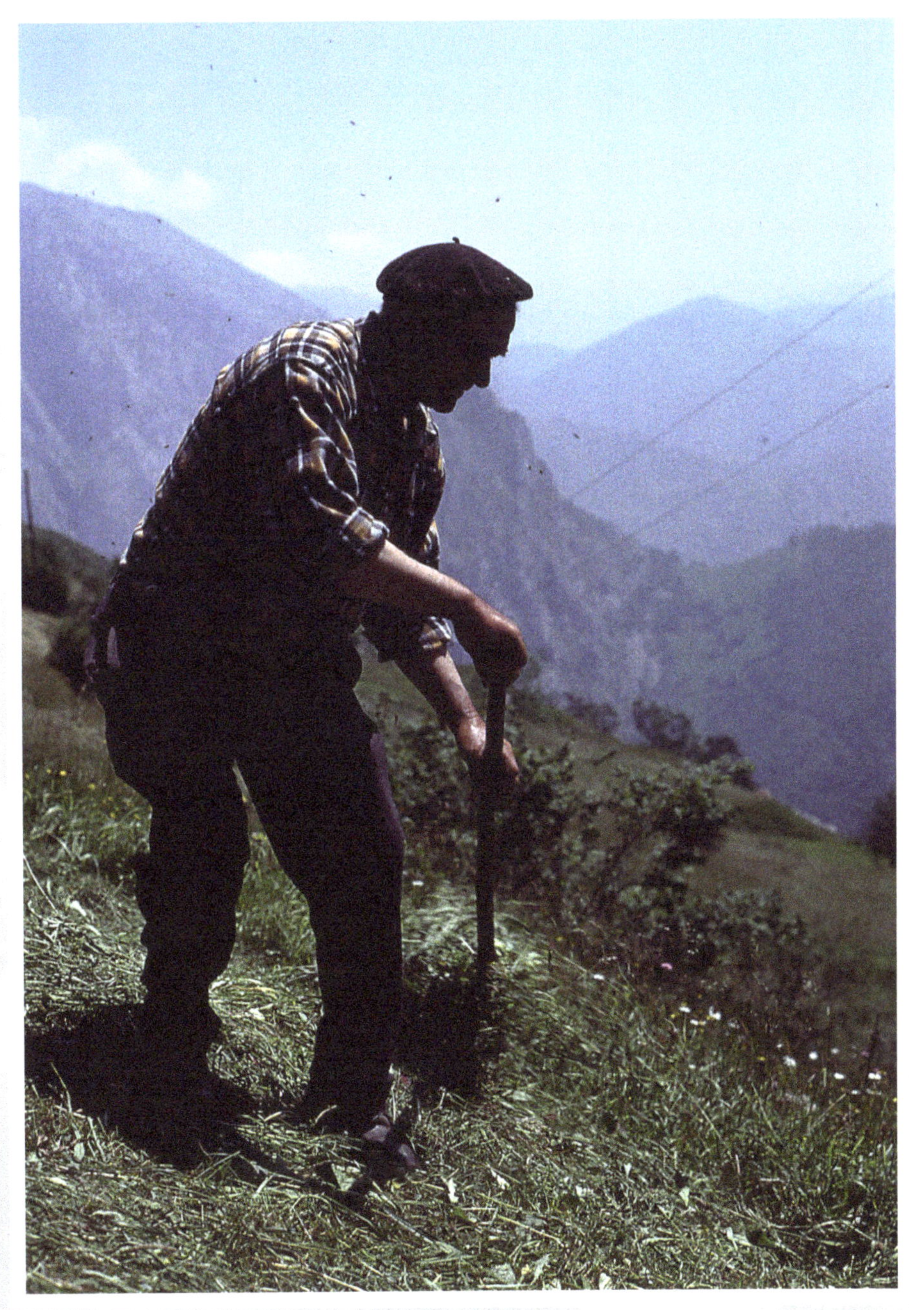

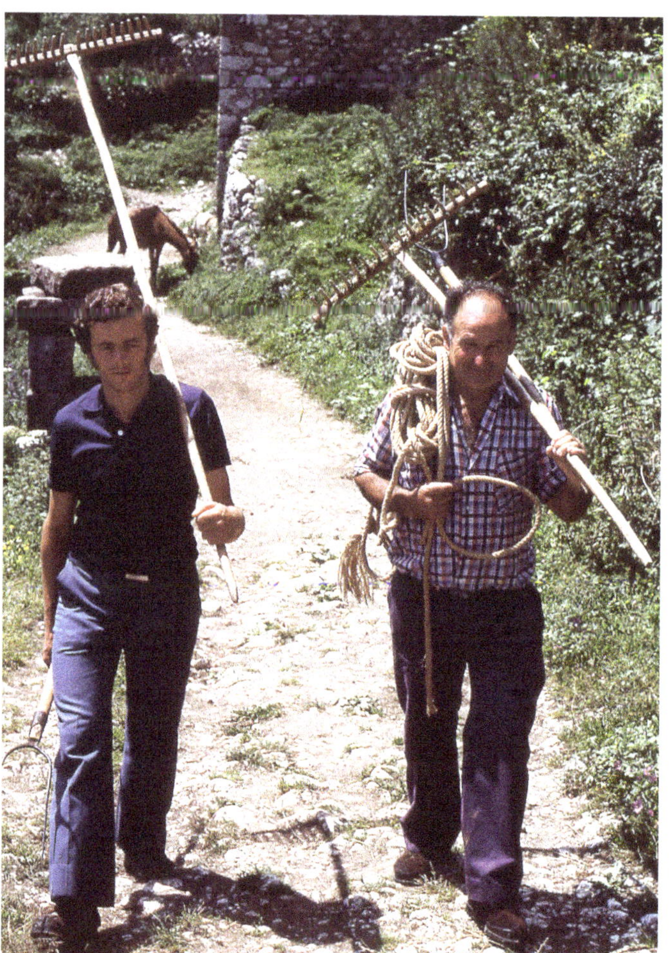

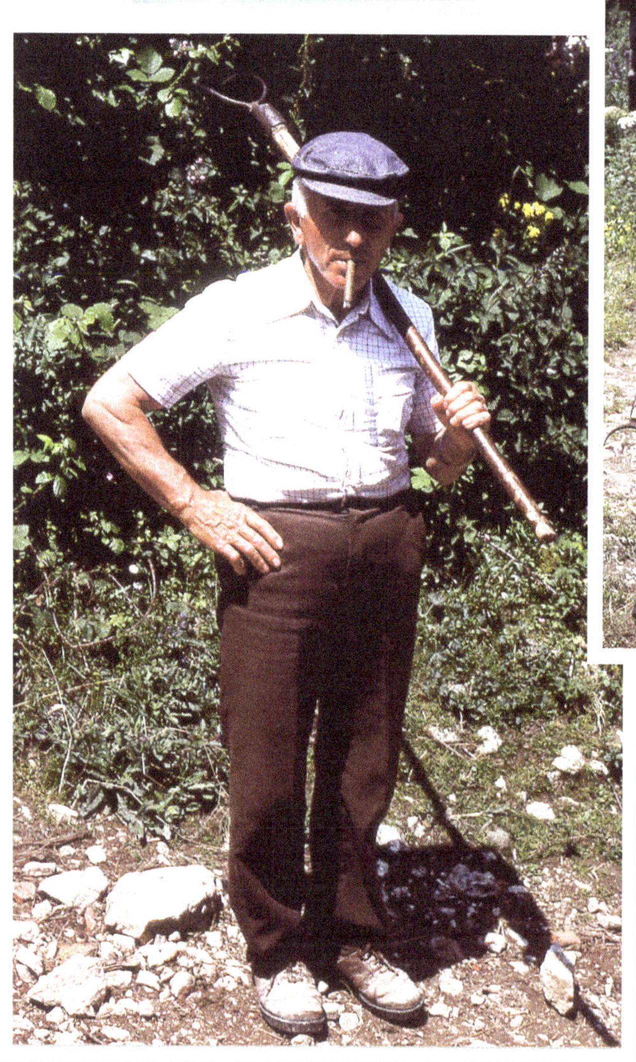

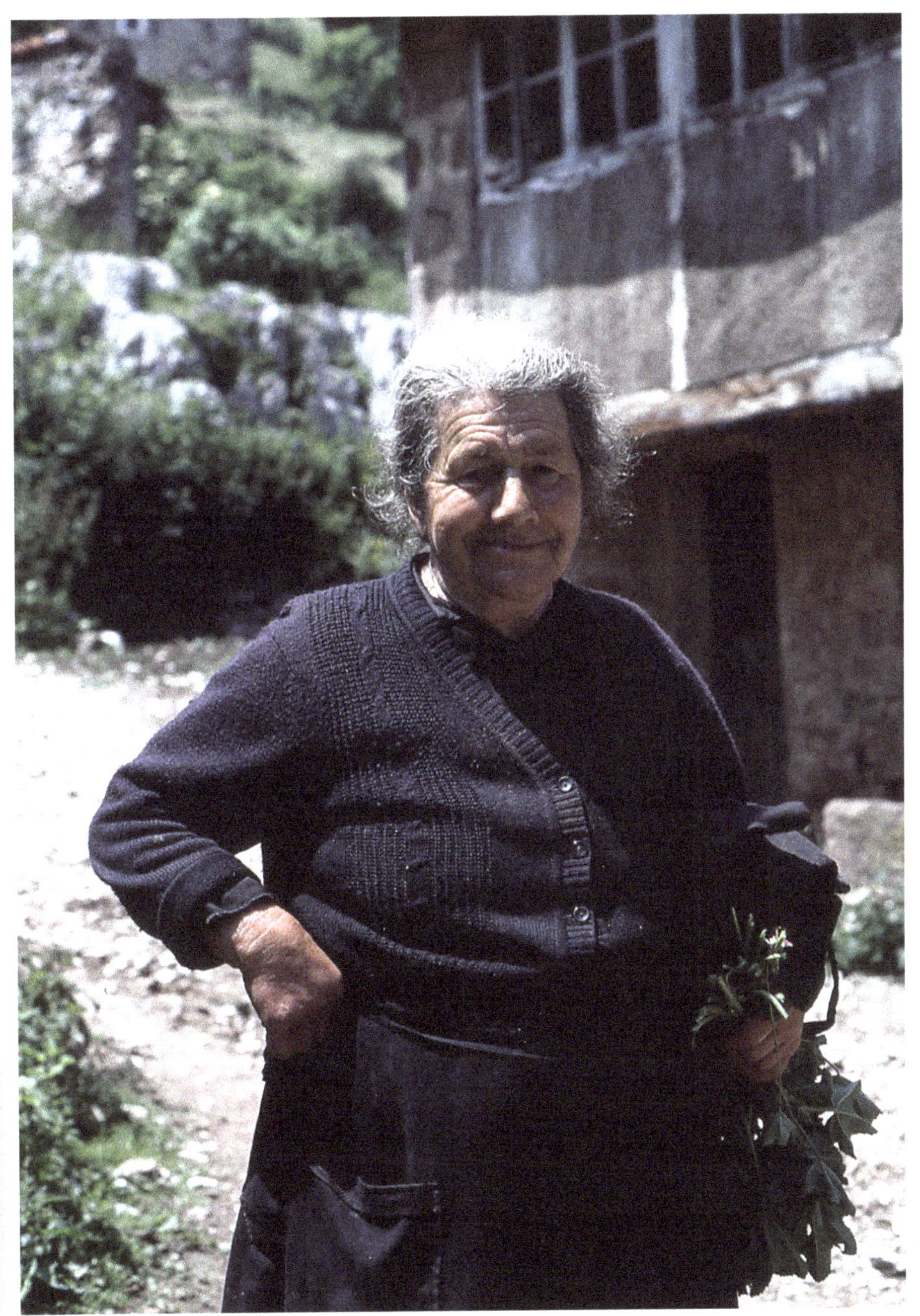

I couldn't see my destination but I trusted the map. In this way I made the ascent—prodding, uncomfortable, footsore. Then everything changed as I saw from a distance small figures working in the fields surrounding the village, and in the background the roof of the village church. I wasn't alone. There really was a Tresviso. It wasn't until I was very close that I noticed how many of the workers were old. Not just "old" to a 30-year old, but old enough to qualify for "senior citizen" status at all those centers in New Mexico. So I photographed old women in long black dresses on hills too steep for long dresses or old women, and made my way to the heart of the village where Jack told me there was a bar where we would meet. When I asked a couple of the younger villagers in my poor Spanish where the bar was, they laughed and pointed to one of the village houses where I found the "bar" was the front room of a modest house, without a sign of any sort.

I entered the bar and ordered a soda—afraid that if I drank a beer I wouldn't be able to handle the return hike, and waited for Jack and Sue. After a few minutes, I felt my legs begin to cramp and I knew I had to keep moving. But before I left, I bought a postcard and a chocolate bar, scribbled a note, and asked the owner to give my message and chocolate to Jack—*el inglés, antiguo pero fuerte* (old but strong). I gestured in the direction I had come, walked my fingers along his bar, and headed back down the trail.

I learned later from Sue that upon entering the empty bar, Jack's face fell. For a few seconds he doubted my resolve and was deeply disappointed. He knew his wife, Barbara, was having health issues, but the young Barbara, who he always called "Strelke," so his Barbaras wouldn't be confused during our hikes, needed to see Tresviso. Soon the owner of the bar presented the note and chocolate. The note, as I recall now, said that I was getting a head start because I was young and slow.

Tresviso was my most memorable hike in the *Picos* and one which I repeated with Don many years later. Now, as I recall that first summer of hiking and look again at photographs, I can see that our hikes in the Pyrenees and our travels through the small towns and valleys there had a different character from the mountains and towns in the

Picos range. If I could write in color, the mountains and high valleys in the *Picos* would be green, gold, and red. Since this range begins closer to sea level, there are more settlements, and I would often see clusters of stone houses with gently sloping clay tile roofs against a verdant landscape.

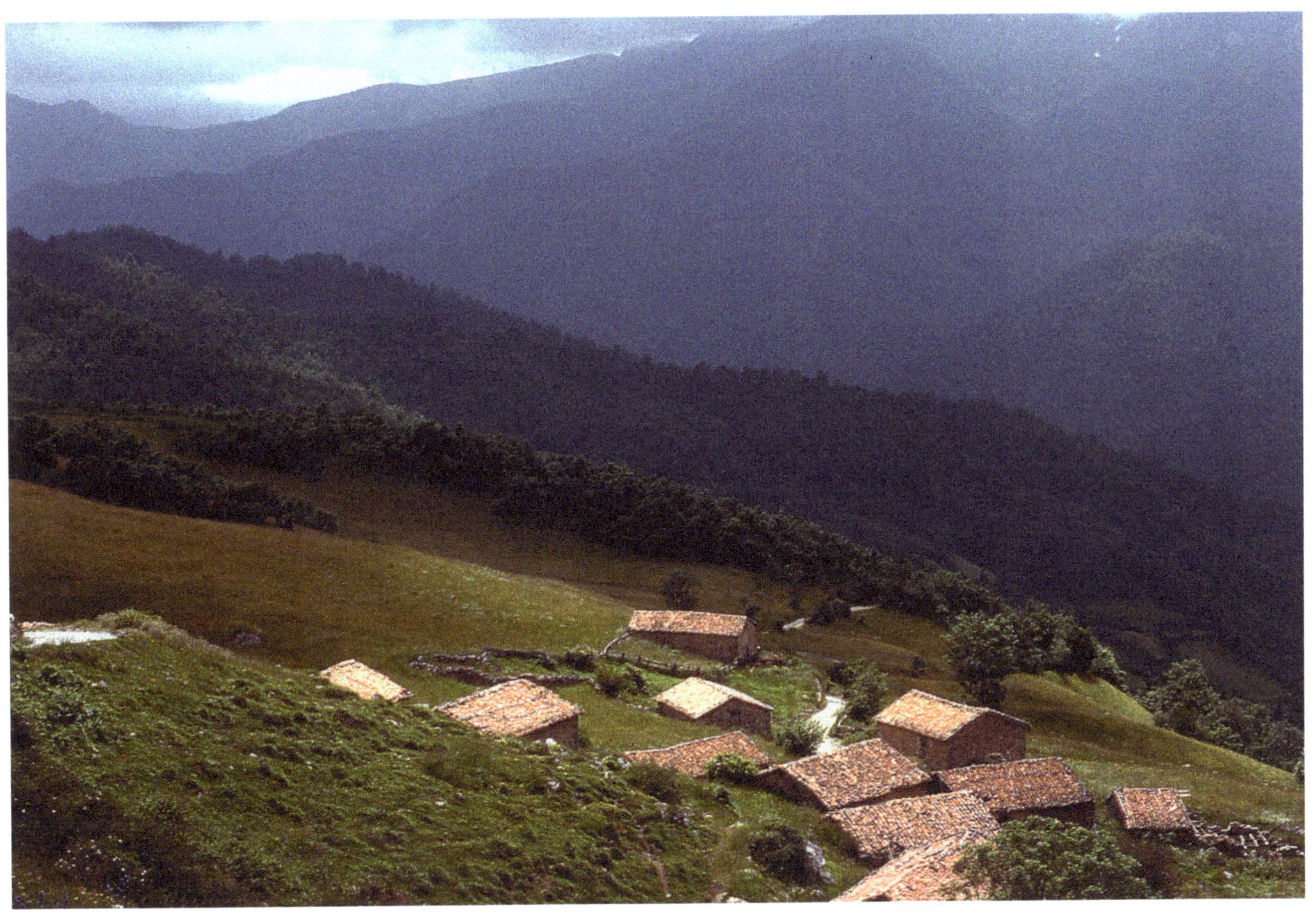

Picos landscape, near Potes, Cantabria

In contrast, my mind's eye associates the high valleys in the Pyrenees with blue, gray, and white. Although the high meadows are green and lush in the summer, towns and villages lie at a higher elevation. Houses are slate-roofed, with a steeper pitch than the clay-roofed houses in the *Picos*. To me the Pyrenean landscape was overwhelming and seemed to lack human scale—what I would later learn in landscape theory as the difference between the sublime and the picturesque.

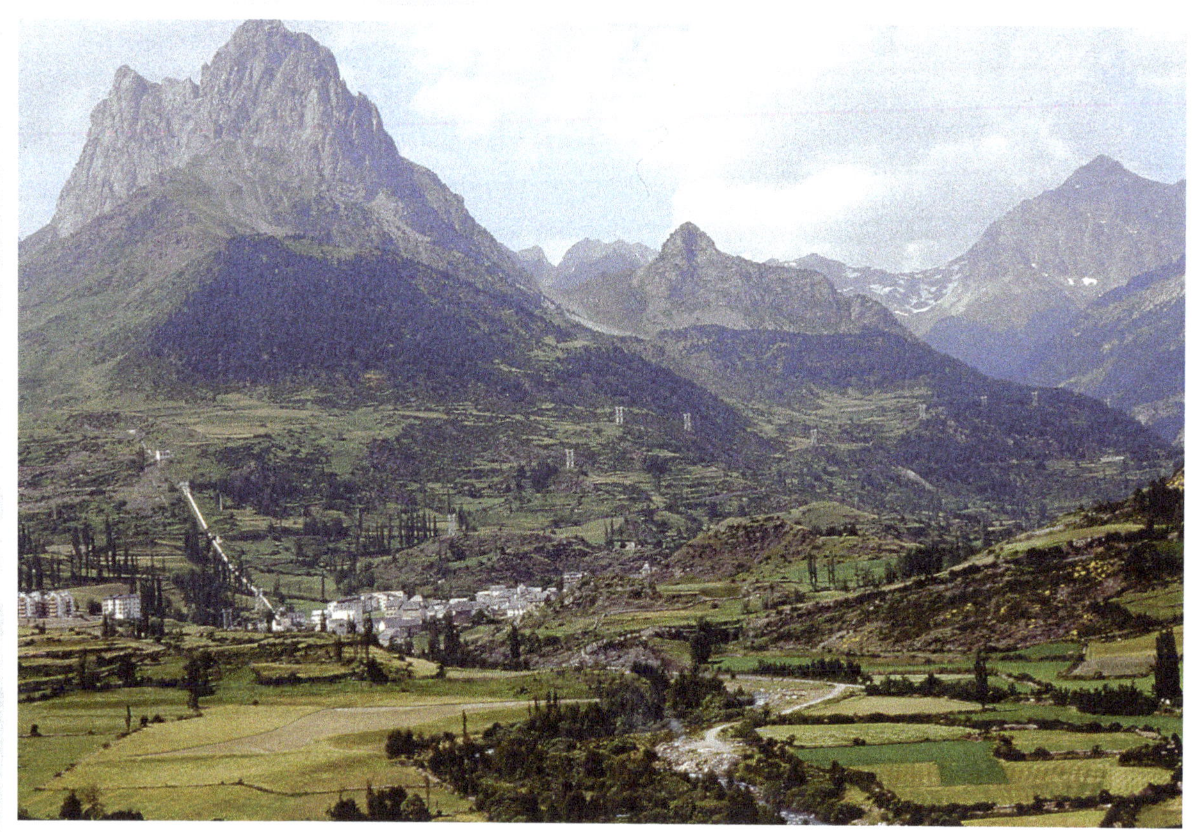

Above Sallent de Gallego, Pyrenees

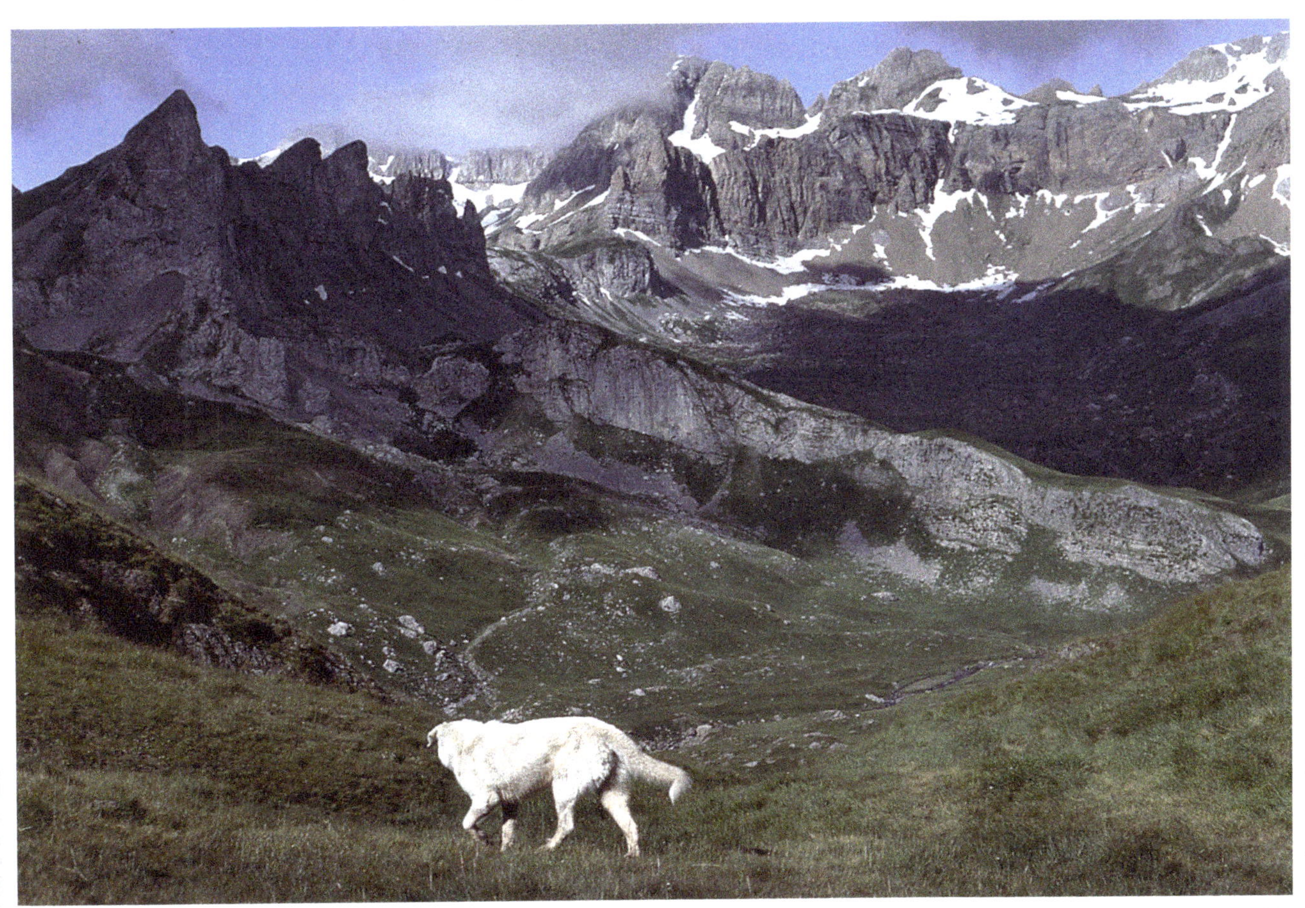

Hiking with Great Pyrenees dog on Escarra trail, Pyrenees

Towns like Torla, at the edge of the Ordesa National Park, were thriving as tourist destinations, but many towns we drove through were in decline, either because of migration to the cities, or because many small towns and villages lost their rural livelihood when dams were built for hydroelectric power and fields were flooded. The poem and photo sequence in the *Homage to Lanuza* chapter of this book responds to my sense of unease and sadness when as an outsider I viewed these deserted villages, or saw the less touristic side of Torla.

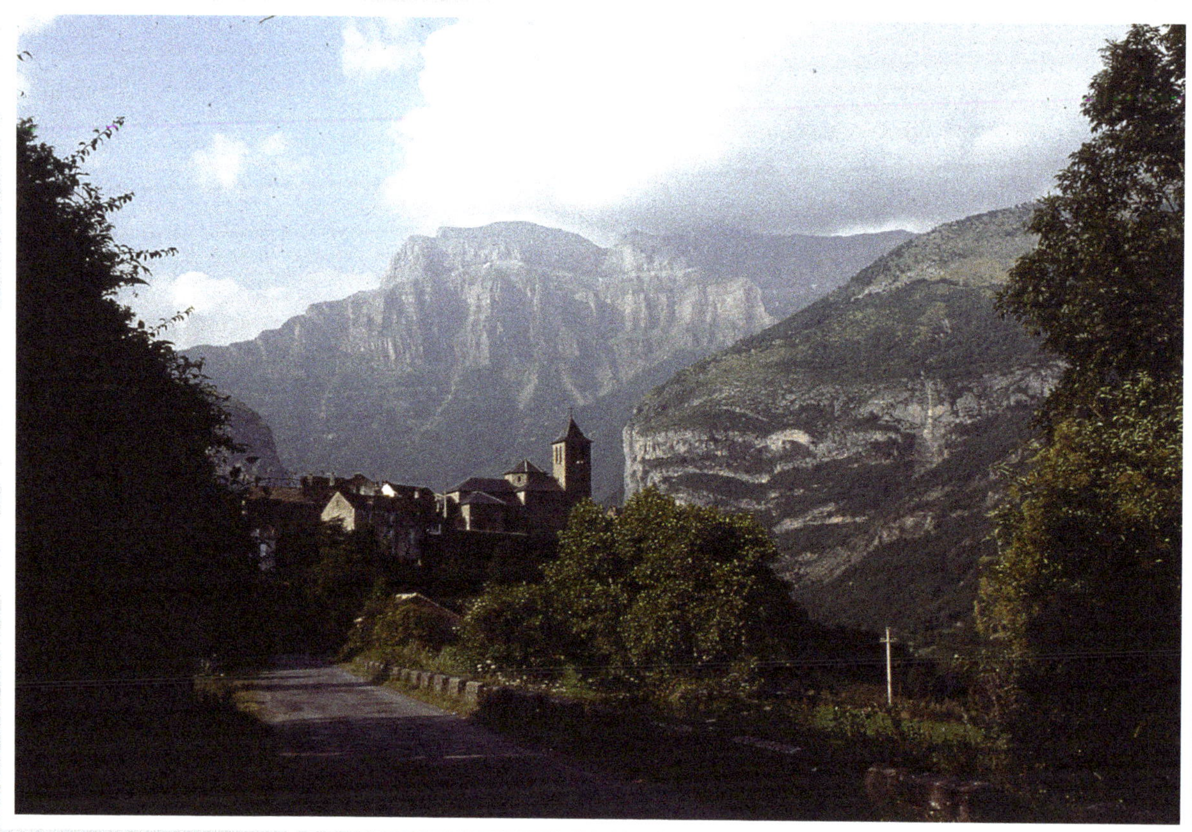

Torla/Ordessa National Park, Province of Huesca, Aragón

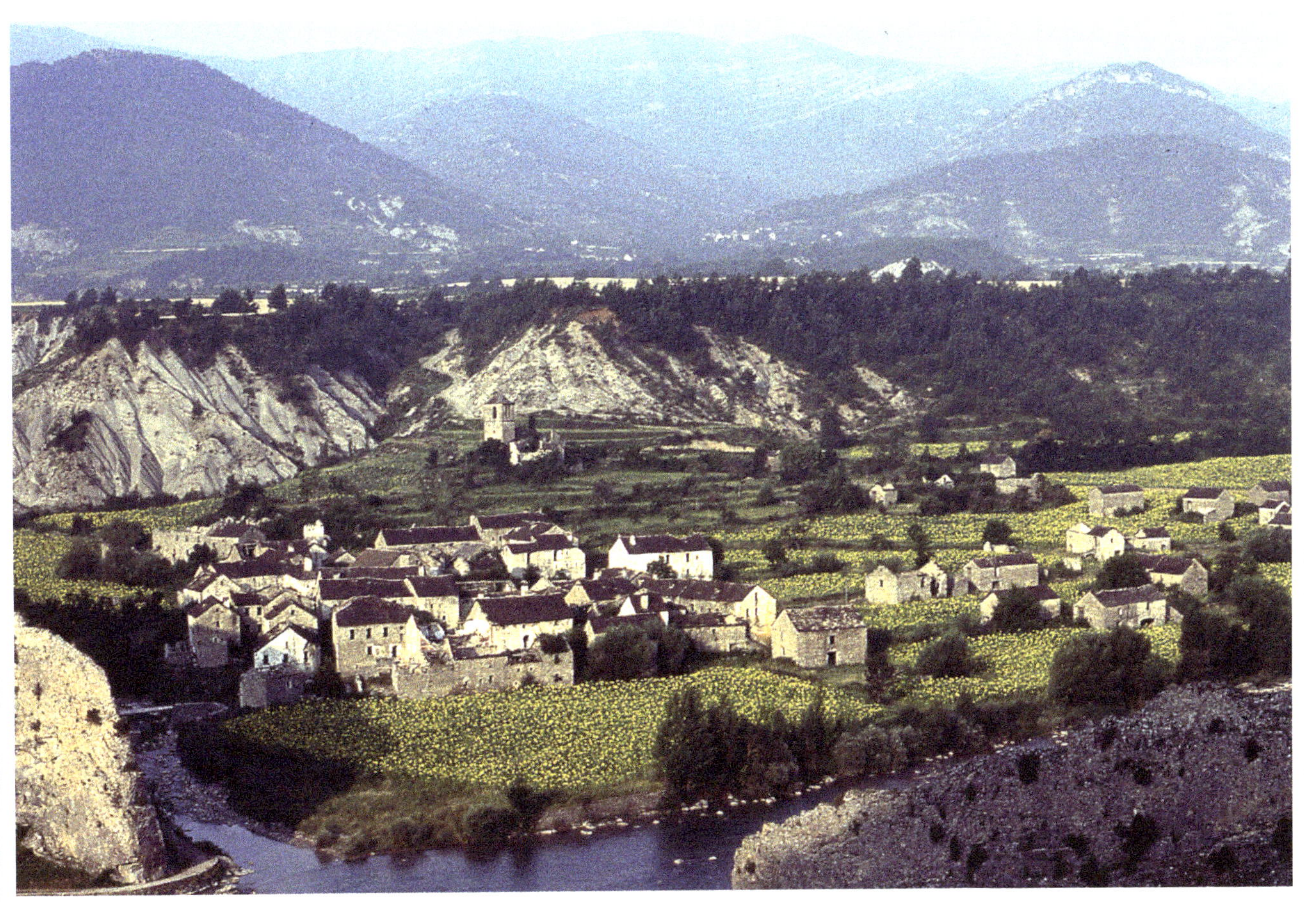

Deserted Village with Sunflowers, Aragón

In 1977 my photographs were taken with a 35mm camera (Pentax Spotmatic) and I used Kodachrome and Ektachrome slide film because many of these images did indeed become a slide show that was viewed at senior centers in New Mexico the following year. The black and white photographs taken that first summer in Spain were taken with a Yashica twin lens reflex camera, using 120 Plus-X or Pan-X roll film.

By the following year when my husband and I returned to spend most of his sabbatical year in Spain, I had upgraded my camera to a Mamiya 645. Although I shot Kodacolor II and Kodacolor 400 film, most of my photographs from this period are black and white (also Pan-X or Plus-X film). I was a serious photographer at the time and developed my own film when possible and always printed my own images in my Albuquerque darkroom.

It was because of my wonderful summer of hiking in northern Spain that Don and I decided to spend most of the following year in Spain. We had started in England, then spent a month in Scandinavia where we bought a car, but Spain was our destination for the winter. We didn't know where we would make our winter home but thought somewhere in the south, maybe the *Costa del Sol* along the Mediterranean. We were in Madrid for a week in early November and visited one of the city tourist offices where we were disappointed to learn that the *Costa del Sol* would be too expensive for our budget. Don was on two-thirds pay and I had resigned my job at the New Mexico Commission on Aging to travel for a year, and we had spent three times our monthly budget while in Sweden and Finland.

The woman at the tourist office pointed to a map of Spain and put her finger on the *Costa de la Luz*, a smaller strip of the Andalusian coast south of Portugal and facing the Atlantic. So we headed to Seville and the *Costa de la Luz*, only to find a very deserted area in what was off-season, with small towns that might have had charm 50 years ago as fishing villages but now were marred by blocks of whitewashed condos that stood along the beach like stiff soldiers at attention. We looked at a condo in the town of Chipiona because our hotel manager in Seville owned a unit there. He had described a penthouse unit with a terraced garden and 360-degree views. What we found was not my imagined palatial ex-pat retreat but a cold and sterile unit with the promised 360-degree view of other dreary and deserted condos, not of the ocean. And where was the town? So we drove south to the *Costa del Sol* and its capital, Malaga, hoping to find both sun and a home for the winter that we could afford—a place where Don could do his math research and writing and where I could photograph and write poetry.

Most of towns we saw near Malaga were high end tourist destinations blighted with stacks of high rise hotels and condos. So we kept heading east, enjoying our drive along the Mediterranean and stopping for a few snapshots.

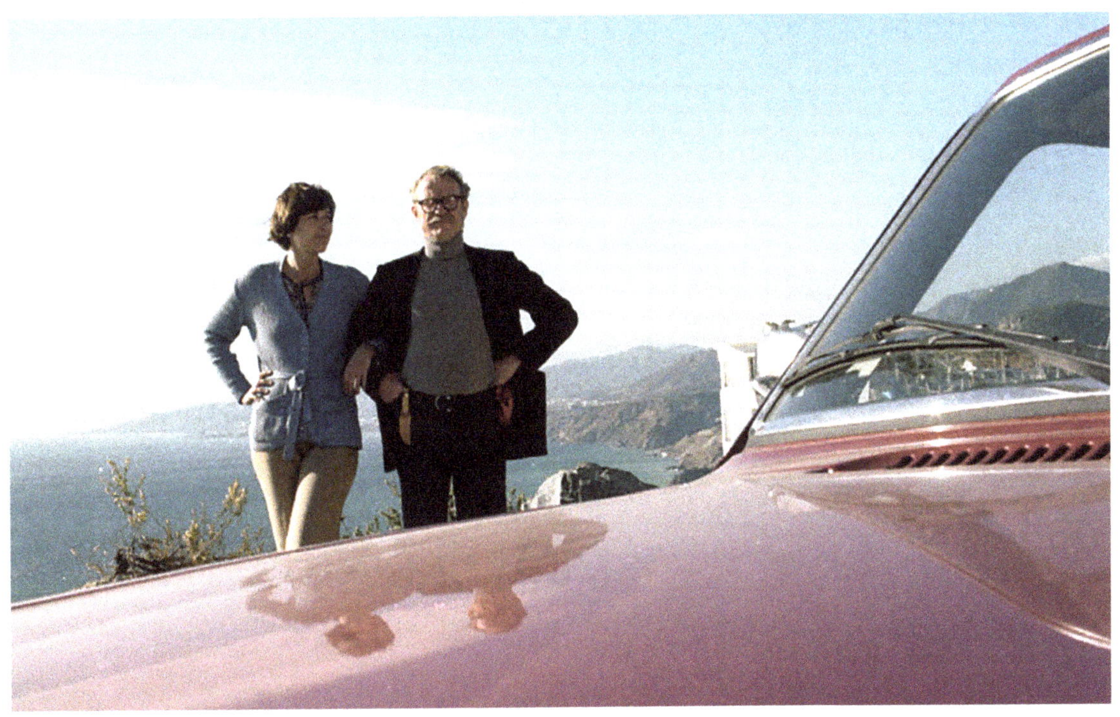

My late husband, Don and I, along the Mediterranean

It was near the end of our second day of driving on the main road to Almería when we came to a road block and detour that looked like it would take us hours to navigate. By this time we were tired, hungry, and disheartened. There was nothing to do but turn back to the nearest town, a small dot on our road map, to find a grocery store and maybe a hotel for the night.

The small town was Almuñecar and just by chance we wandered down to the seaside promenade, the *malecón,* where we saw a real estate sign and decided to investigate. The office was run by Jose Cordero, a handsome young man who stuffed us into his red sports car and whipped us down the beach road to look at two condos. It was a scene out of *To Catch a Thief* with me as Grace Kelly—silk scarf trailing in the sea breeze as she raced along the French Riviera with Cary Grant (and I had Jose Cordero—Joe Lamb—and Don). Both units were less than half the price the tourist office in Madrid had predicted. In fact, when Jose said the monthly rent *pesetas* equivalent of $150, we thought he was telling us the weekly rent. We had found our home for the next six months, a one-bedroom condo with two balconies that overlooked the beach and fishing boats. We would each have a lovely balcony "office" that we termed our *balcón de trabajo,* our work balcony.

Almuñecar was infatuation at first sight and as we lived there my feelings for the town and the *Costa Tropical* deepened. It had a belt of midrise condos and clay-roofed new patio homes for ex-pats, but there was a heart to the town. I loved the relaxed lifestyle of our ex-pat haven and never tired of looking at and photographing fisherman bringing in their nets, the jumble of houses in the old town, and people going about their daily business. As I remember the place now, I can picture a panoramic sweep of sea, headlands and coves, the green of banana, sugar cane, and cherimoya crops and, further inland, terraces of almond trees.

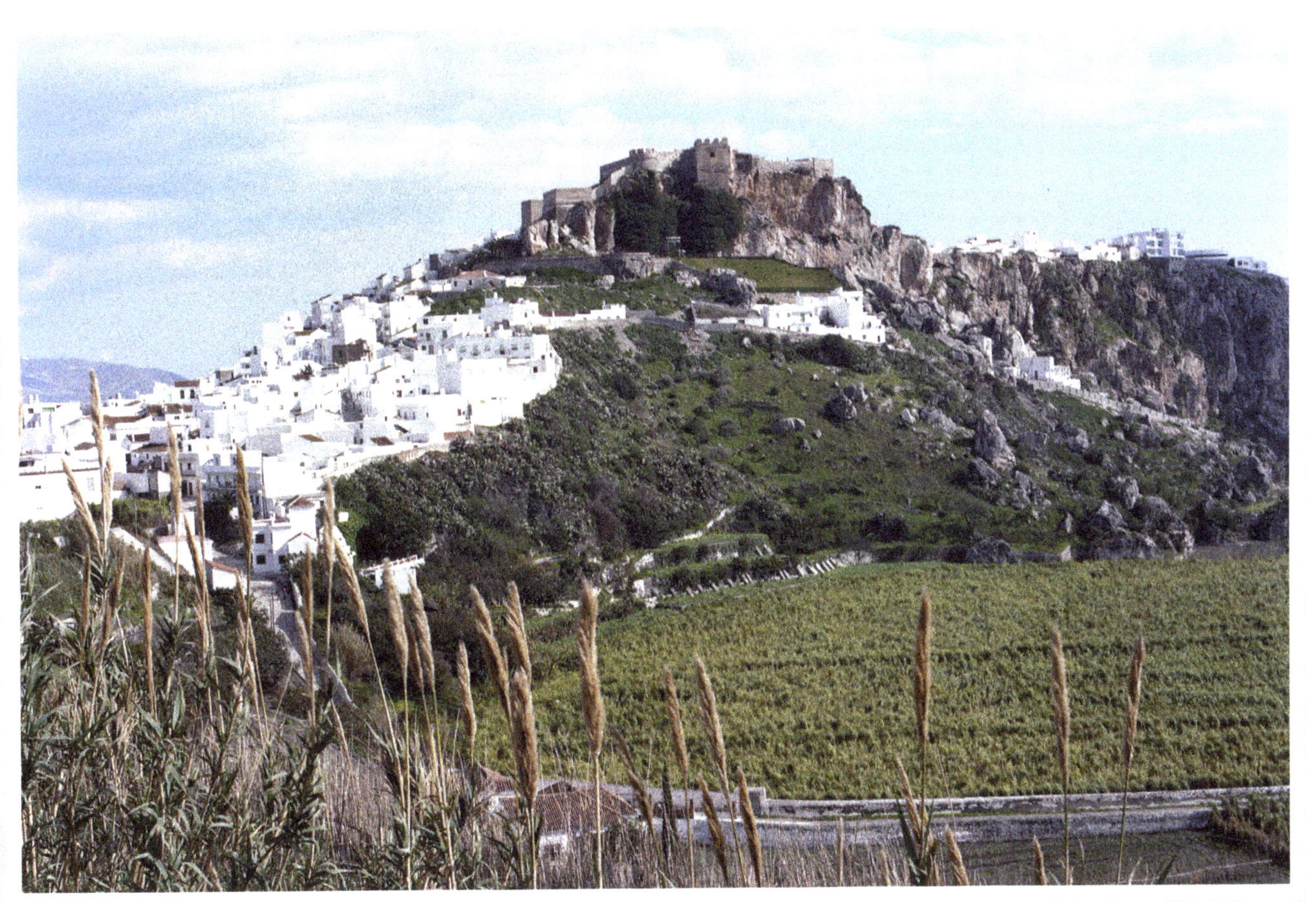

Salobreña with Moorish castle, Province of Granada, Andalusia

The town's natural beauty was matched by its cultural history. Almuñecar was first settled by the Phoenicians, then came the Romans, with a fortress, aqueducts and ruins as evidence. By the 8th century it was a thriving Moorish town, with a maze of narrow streets and whitewashed houses built in the old town. By the late 15th century, the Christian era brought another layer of town heritage. The *Calle Real*, royal road, cut straight up into the old Moorish quarter where my favorite butcher shop stood not more than five meters from the town's 16th century royal fountain.

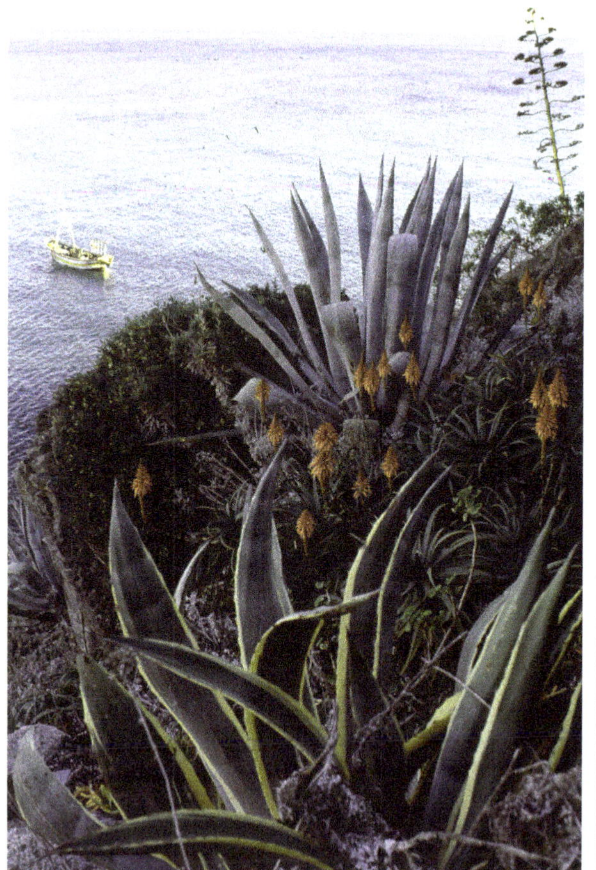

Agave and sea, Almuñecar, Province of Granada

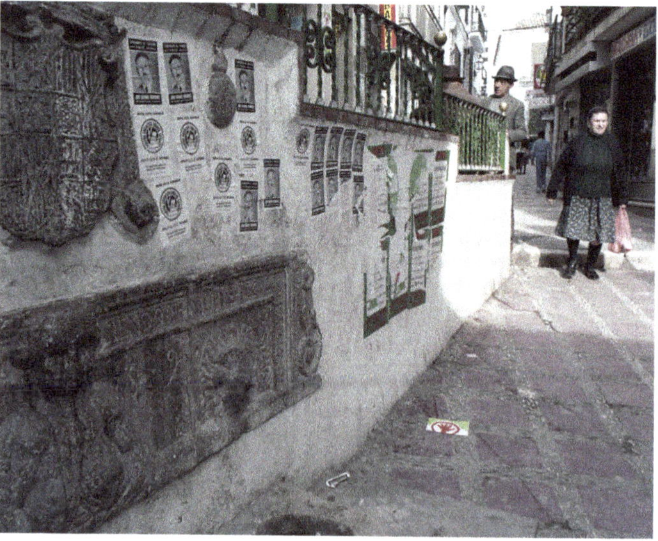

Royal fountain and street in Old Town, Almuñecar

I returned again and again to the castle that stood on the bluff overlooking the sea, at first to photograph the ramparts with the sea in the background, or the closer view of the modern town that appeared to have tumbled at the castle's feet. Later I photographed the cemetery that was within the castle grounds and constructed like a miniature apartment complex. Graves were stacked in rows above ground rather than buried—niche graves in high walls, giving the appearance of a small city of the dead. It was a troubling place in many ways, built after a cholera epidemic in the late 19th century and, as with many Spanish cemeteries I saw in the late 1970s, somewhat neglected and in disrepair. In spite of a level of discomfort with photographing in what felt like a private place, I visited often and would look over the rampart walls toward Africa and wonder at my good fortune. My *Village of Dreams* poem gives a sense of my ambivalence. I learned years later when I visited Almuñecar that the cemetery had been moved in 1986 to permit restoration of the castle. Many of the photographs in the *Village of Dreams* chapter are from this cemetery and the nearby village of Salobreña.

Our time in Spain included day trips in Andalusia but also one or two trips to Madrid. During one such trip Don spent the day in the university library, researching math reviews, and I ventured off by train to Segovia and Ávila. I thought I would be the one to have adventures to tell, but when I returned to the hotel that evening it was Don who had the most exciting news. He was recognized, as if picked out of the math lineup of internationally renowned researchers. He wondered how was it possible since he taught at a second-rate university and researched in an obscure specialty of real algebraic geometry. Yet, miracles happen. Another miracle that I associate with Spain.

He had been standing at the librarian's desk, requesting math volumes, battling communication in Spanglish, and identifying himself as Professor Dubois from the University of New Mexico, when he was overheard by a young man at an adjacent table who blurted out "not Don Dubois!" The young man was Tomás Recio, one of a handful of mathematicians in Spain researching in the same field. Don was so excited with the encounter that he had brought Tomás back to the hotel where he was waiting in the bar to meet me. After a few minutes of formal introductions, I told Tomás I had hiked up to Tresviso the previous summer. His jaw dropped and he asked "Is that right? Not Tresviso! ¡Increíble!" Now as I recall that evening, I am smiling to myself because for the next nearly 40 years of our friendship, whenever Tomás was incredulous or surprised, he would begin by asking "Is that right? ¡Increíble!"

This chance meeting, a lucky encounter on Valentine's Day, 1979, marked the beginning of 20 years of mathematics collaboration between Don and Tomás. That first evening we talked about personal histories, our travels, hiking, poetry, and math. Tomás was a gifted mathematician and professor at the Complutense University of Madrid. When we met he was only 26-years old and already a Renaissance man—a scholar, hiker, naturalist, poet, amateur historian, and fluent in English and French.

During the following few days we met Tomás' wife, Isabel, and two of Tomás' most promising math students, Carlos and Victor, who would both study with Don in Albuquerque the following year. Currently Rector of the Complutense University of Madrid, Carlos Andradas finished his Ph.D. in New Mexico with Don as his advisor and returned to Spain to begin an illustrious career as a research mathematician, educator, and administrator.

This story is a sidebar, perhaps a tangential story of Don's professional life, but it is part of my-life-in-Spain story as well. It isn't necessary to help one appreciate the poems or photographs in this book but it explains why for many years we were able to return to Spain and how my friendship with Tomás, Isabel, Cristina—their best friend, and Carlos and his wife, Lina, is part of my love affair with Spain.

It was because of our love of Spain and our Spanish friends that Don and I returned to hike in the Picos and Pyrenees. Nearly ten years after that first hike to Tresviso, I had a chance to share the experience with Don as we walked with Tomás and Isabel and their young sons up the six miles of switchbacks and steep terrain to Tresviso. Halfway up the mountain we were engulfed by fog and at times could hardly see the trail.

When we neared trail's end, the fog lifted and we saw the clay rooftops in the distance. Tresviso was still a sleepy village with a population of old people. But at the only village "bar," the same bar from years earlier, and still unsigned, we met teenagers from Los Angeles who were visiting their grandparents. There was a TV blaring a local soccer match, and a mingling of English and Spanish.

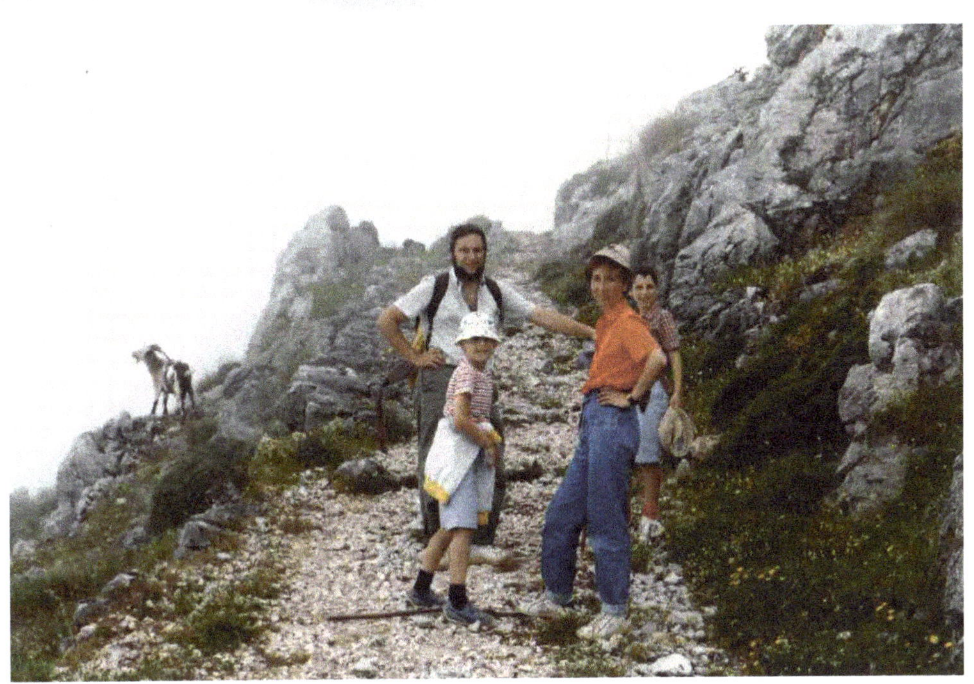

Tomás and Isabel with their young sons, Tresviso trail, 1985

Don took early retirement soon after and I changed careers, from teaching to landscape architecture. We moved to Tucson in 1988 and spent several years together exploring, hiking, and botanizing in the Sonoran desert and the "Sky Islands" that flank the Tucson valley. There was a satisfying new career as a land use planner and urban designer for me, a new home, and new trails to hike in the Santa Catalinas. At the same time, I felt the heavy weight of Don's battle with Alzheimer's and eventual death from cancer in 1997.

If you live long enough, your life is a series of peaks and pits, and from the long lens of time, you have foggy memories of the journey to climb up or climb out. Grieving and hiking have much in common. In the initial phase of mourning, you walk in a fog, go through the motions of work, family, and friends. At least that's how I see it now, as I recall some of my most challenging hikes and the first year after my husband's death. It's one foot in front of the other.

Hiking was my boot camp, my preparation for battles without a declared war, my preparation for life. When I needed to be brave and move forward through the fog of grieving and sorrow, I would think of difficult things I had done: walking from the Grand Canyon rim to the Colorado River and back in one long day, finishing a Ph.D., losing 30 lbs after I had gotten fat and soft, hiking to Tresviso twice. So I would survive the first days of mourning, then the first year.

After moving my darkroom three times (in 1981, 1985, and 1988), I finally packed it up and shoved it into a Tucson closet and started to paint. Then in 2004 when I was remodeling the studio in my Tucson house, I found the boxes of photographic equipment and my Omega enlarger (wrapped carefully and in perfect shape). One of the workers was a young photographer who had just won a photo award in his senior year in high school. I recall that he was actually the neighbor of my worker and he was only there one day. A good day for him to pitch in since he looked at my antiquated equipment with love in his eyes, and I gave it all to him. I told him the only price was an invitation to his first photography exhibit.

Over the years I returned to Spain many times. As Jack had introduced Spain to me, I in turn could do so to friends who I hope would relish the maps, photos, stories and anecdotes as much as I did years before. I returned with my second husband in 2010 and, in Santander, introduced Charlie to Tomás and Isabel, and in Madrid to Carlos, Lina, and Cristina.

When I first met Tomás and Isabel in 1979, they were young parents of two sons who Tomás would lead on his treks in the mountains. Now their grandchildren are old enough to hike in the *Picos*. Charlie and I explored new territory together in the *Rioja* and *Picos* and returned again in 2013 and 2016 to visit our Spanish friends and see new places together. Although we had all changed with age, the iconic Osborne bull, undoubtedly the most photographed billboard in Spain, was a constant presence in the Spanish landscape.

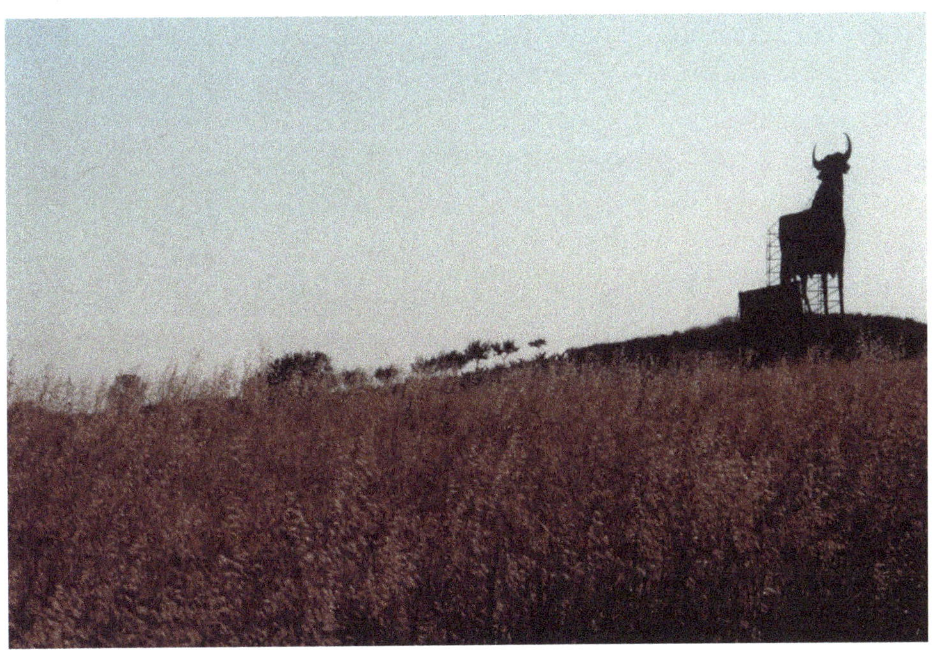

Osborne bull billboard

In 2016 our good friend, Caroline Durand, made our traveling threesome. While Charlie walked on the northern route of the *Camino de Santiago*, from Santander to Llanes and beyond, Caroline and I were his car back-up. While he contemplated what pilgrims contemplate, to the tinkle of cows bells and the distant sounds of the sea, Caroline and I were relaxed tourists along the route. Santillana del Mar and the caves of Altamira had changed with the passage of time. In 1977, although access was controlled and we had to wear boots and raincoats, Jack, Barbara, Sue, and I were able to visit the actual Altamira cave and see the astounding paintings of bison and deer made by early artists nearly 20,000 years earlier. I recall I had to lean and sway and stoop to see that the contours of the rock modeled the flanks and contours of the animals. Someone has called Altamira the "Sistine Chapel of prehistoric art," but this seems trite or too glib, for Altamira is more visceral, elemental, and frightening.

In 2010 Charlie and I had visited the museum replica at Altamira, not the actual cave but a beautifully designed scale model of the cave itself. In 2016, while Charlie was walking between Santander and Santillana del Mar, Caroline and I visited small villages and then drove to Santillana, parked in one of the many car parks that surround the medieval town, now a major tourist destination, and waited at a cafe on the route of St. James. Charlie had to pass our sidewalk table and see us sipping our *cañas* of beer and munching olives.

It is a joy to revisit places and reconnect with friends. With the passage of time, I want to celebrate that time of trekking and 20-mile per day hikes. Is "celebration" really another word for nostalgia? I don't think so. I'm not pining for that time because those adventures are being replaced with others equally enjoyable and enlightening, albeit new places explored at a more relaxed pace.

The photographs and poems, unless otherwise noted, are from the late 1970s. Francisco Franco, *El Caudillo*, the military dictator since 1939, had died in 1975 and the country began its transition toward a constitutional monarchy under King Juan Carlos. But there were vestiges of authoritarian rule and loyalty to its dead dictator. It wasn't uncommon in the villages at that time to see *Viva Franco* painted on walls, competing for attention with campaign posters for local candidates and their political parties. By the fall of 1978, while I was happily writing poems and photographing fishermen in Almuñecar, the *Cortes,* the Spanish parliament, was drafting a new constitution.

In December the constitution was approved by nearly 90% of voters in a nationwide referendum. This momentous journey to democracy coincided with great demographic changes as the young people in the countryside continued an unrelenting march to the cities, leaving many of the customs and vestiges of rural life behind. In 1986 Spain entered the European Union, refuting quite literally the anti-Spanish saying, "Europe ends at the Pyrenees." Pan-European political diversity, infrastructure, and regulations have forever changed the country.

Jack saw it coming a decade before in the Pyrenean town of Torla. We had been hiking in the Ordesa National Park by day and in the evening we would stroll the small town and chat with the locals. One night, in the middle of the night, we were awakened by a cacophony of barking dogs, clanging bells, and what sounded like thunder. But it was a clear night under a full moon and we were seeing from our hotel balconies the shadowy parade of hundreds of sheep on the town's main road. There was a chorus of yells and whistles, and some of the shepherds waved to us as they worked to keep their animals moving to the high pastures above the town. Jack and Barbara looked at me from their adjacent balcony and Jack said with a catch in his voice, "this is the Spain I love, the Spain I won't see much longer." As I recall this now, I feel a sad irony in Jack's premonition, for not only was Spain changing and becoming modern and "too European," but Jack was changing. Soon his heart condition would interfere with hiking in Spain and within five years of our wonderful summer, Jack would be dead. It was the classic aftermath of heart surgery: the operation was a success and the patient died.

The Spain I am sharing in these poems and photographs in many ways is Jack's Spain: the Spain of shepherds, road-menders, and fishermen, and of old women in black, forever mourning. It is the Spain of the late 1970s, before the European Union, Facebook, and Twitter. It was a country awakening to democracy and endless opportunities after a long dictatorship. It is my Spain, a place captured in time.

Homage to Lanuza

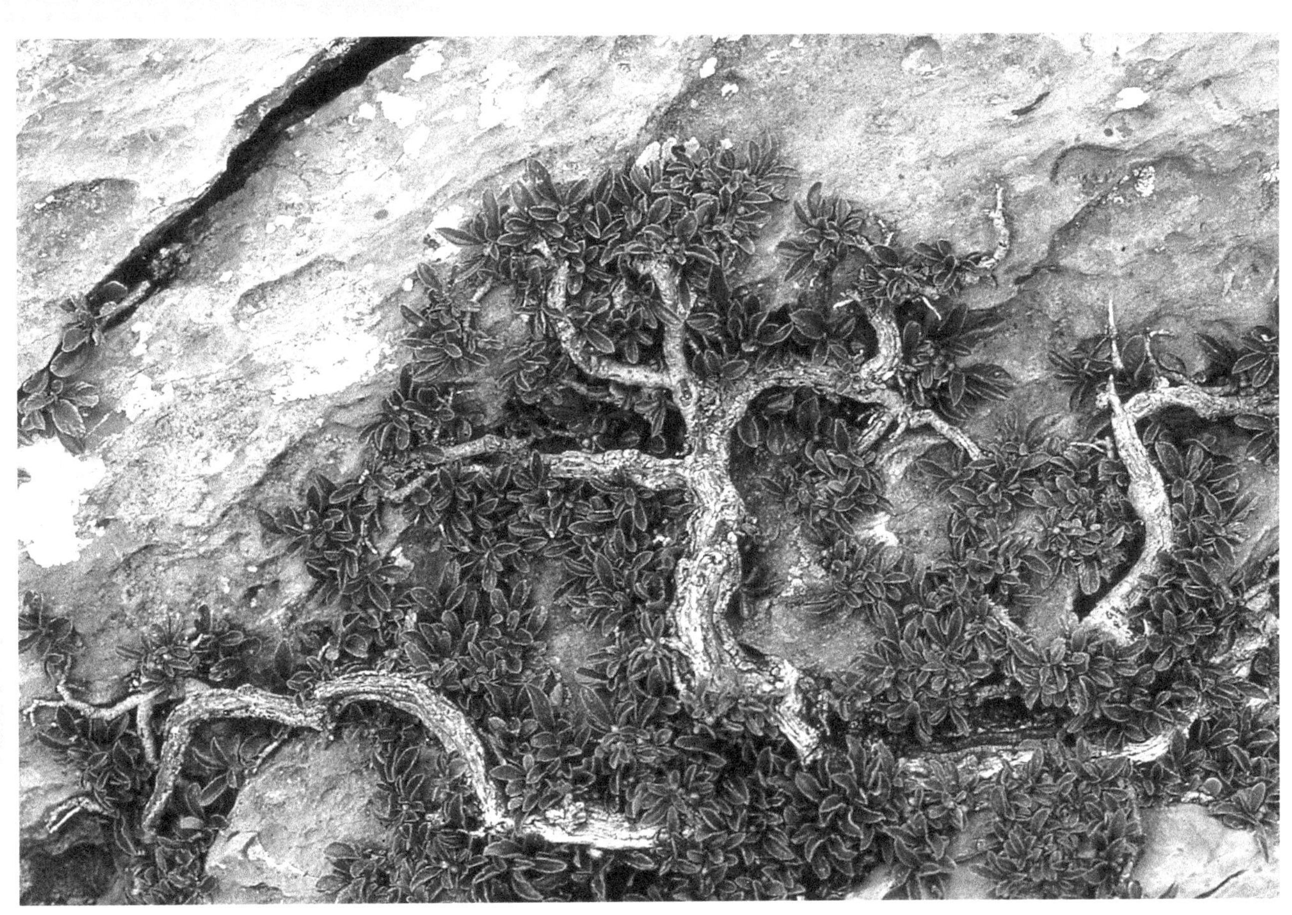

Weeks Before the Flooding of Lanuza, A Pyrenean Village

Its stones are resting now.
Streets deserted.
Houses, carved from mountain slopes,
Roofed with slate,
empty, locked and boarded.
Alleys, quiet in the still, birdless air,
shadowed by stone walls,
cold to the touch:
bluestone.
Cobbles as slick as old crusted snow:
deadstone.
Silhouetted against the autumn sky,
angle of roofs, walls, church tower,
a challenge to weather and rotting time.

I walk across the meadow above Lanuza to see the dam,
the coming of the water, and find another Spanish village.

Homage to Lanuza

Its fields were flooded long ago.
Its buildings, ransacked each summer,
stand just above the waterline:
alive with bits of paper,
stink of garbage and human waste,
fouled spring, rusting trough;
loose shingles flap in the hollow wind.
Its stones are sealing wounds with salt.
Lichens and wild flowers cover walls.
Vines, in retreat, crawl up and over broken windows
into dark sheds.

Lanuza will drown
in the final mountain spring
and remain clean, cold:
hidden, its brood of fins will swim
through windows,
through houses,
through rock to the center of the wet, dark, turning earth.
Fish eyes in skulls of grinning stone.

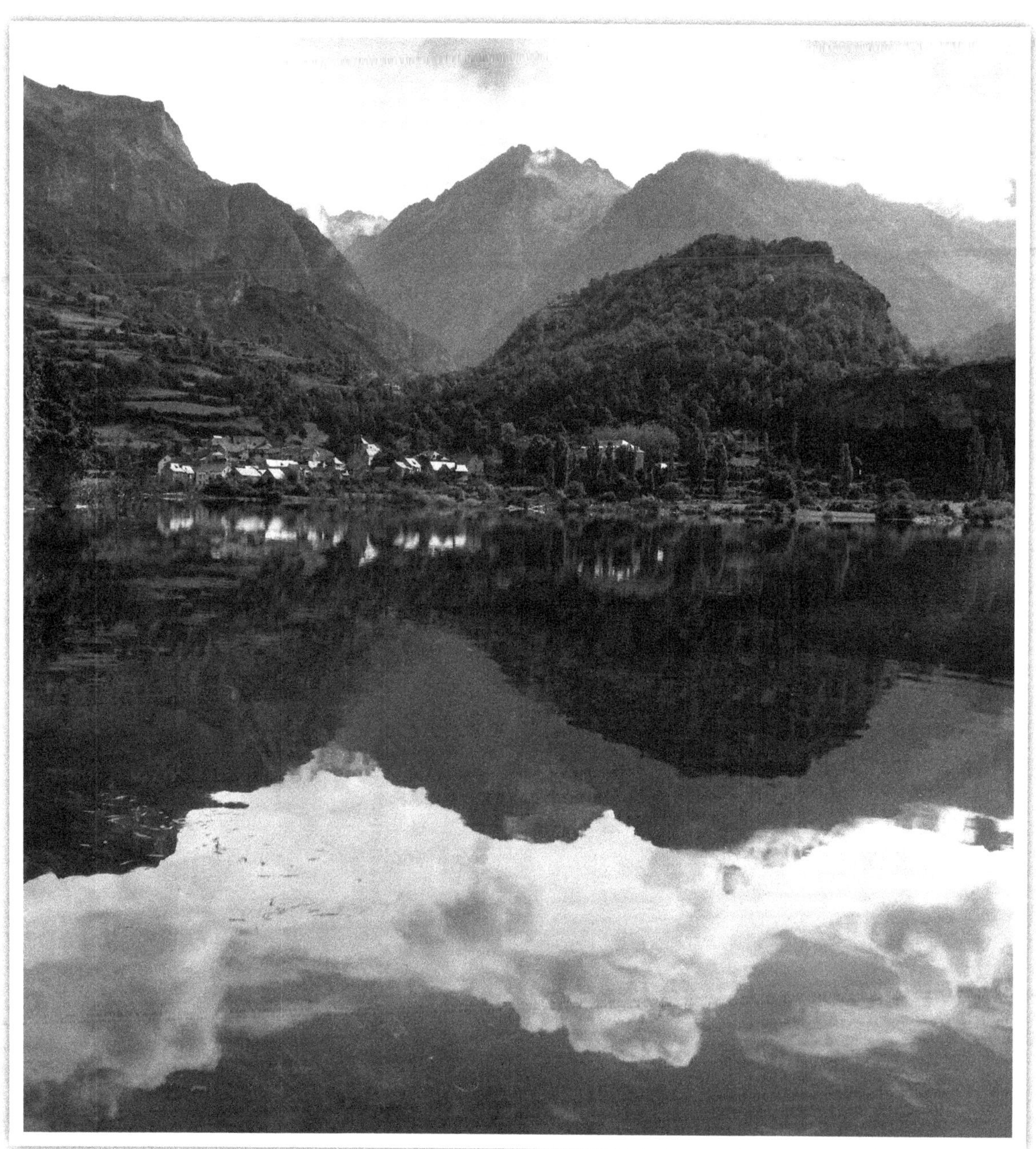

Embalse de Bubal, Province of Huesca, Aragón

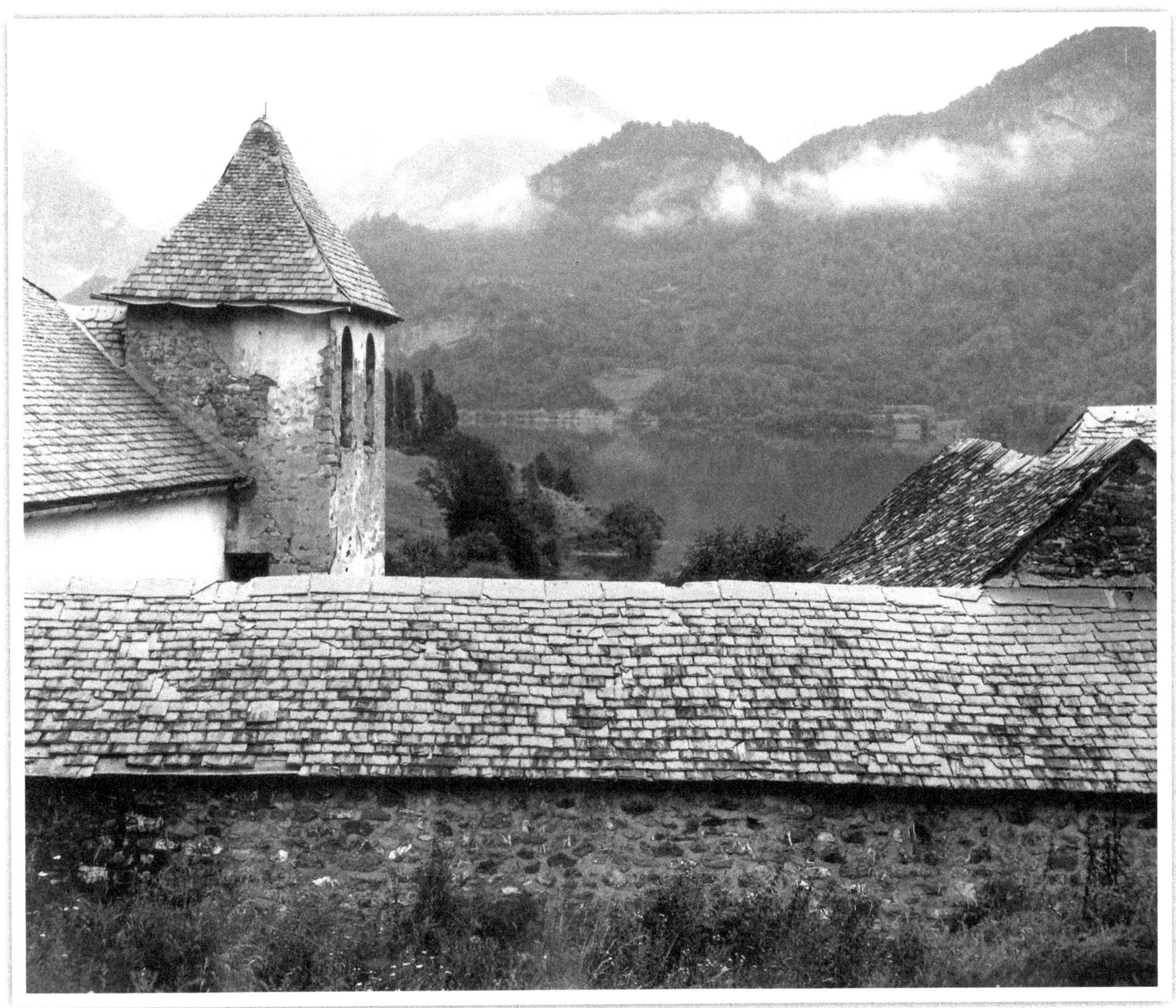

Saques, Province of Huesca, Aragón

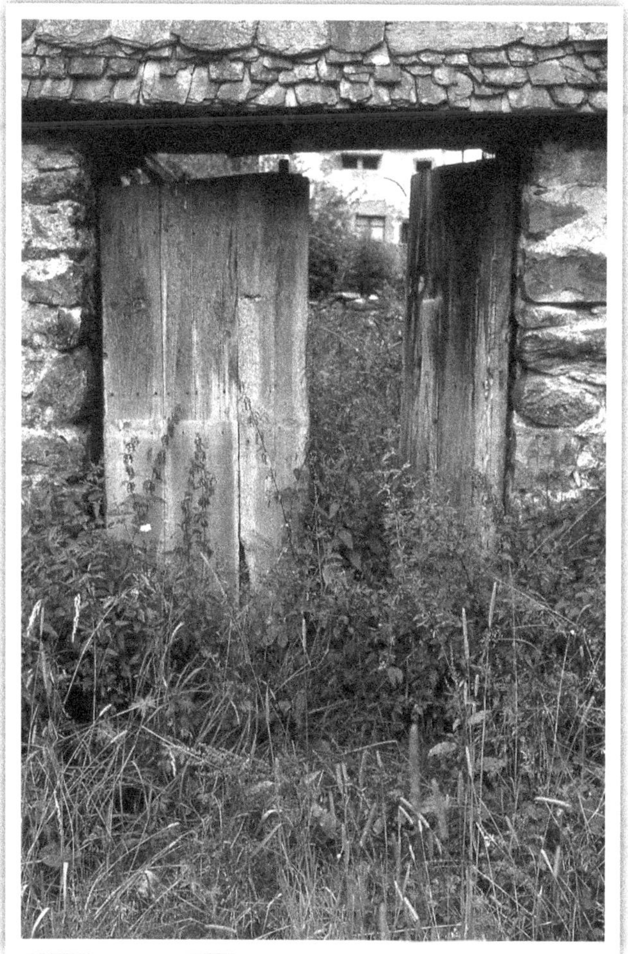

Bubal, Province of Huesca, Aragón

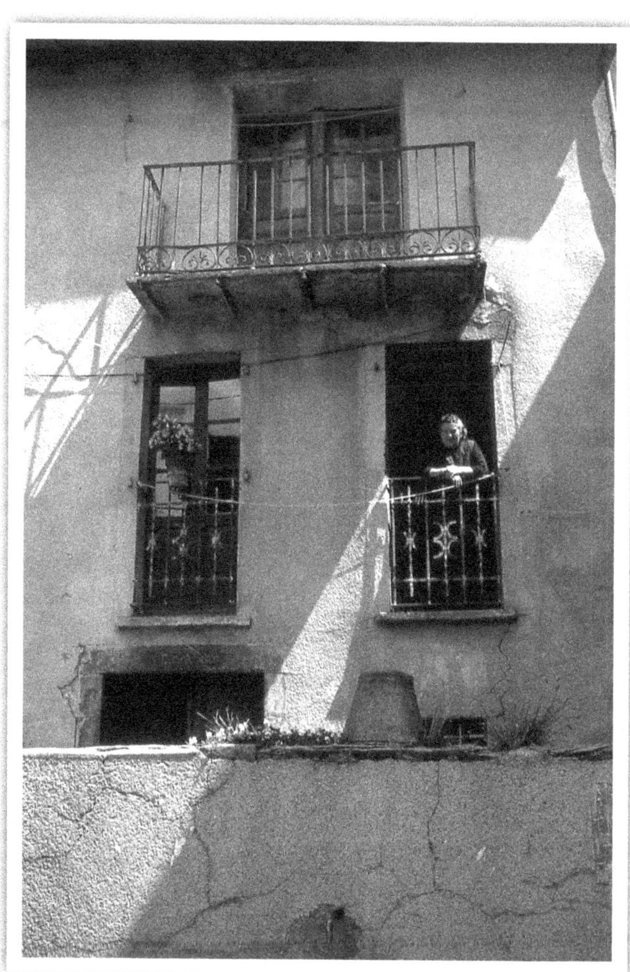

Lanuza, Province of Huesca, Aragón

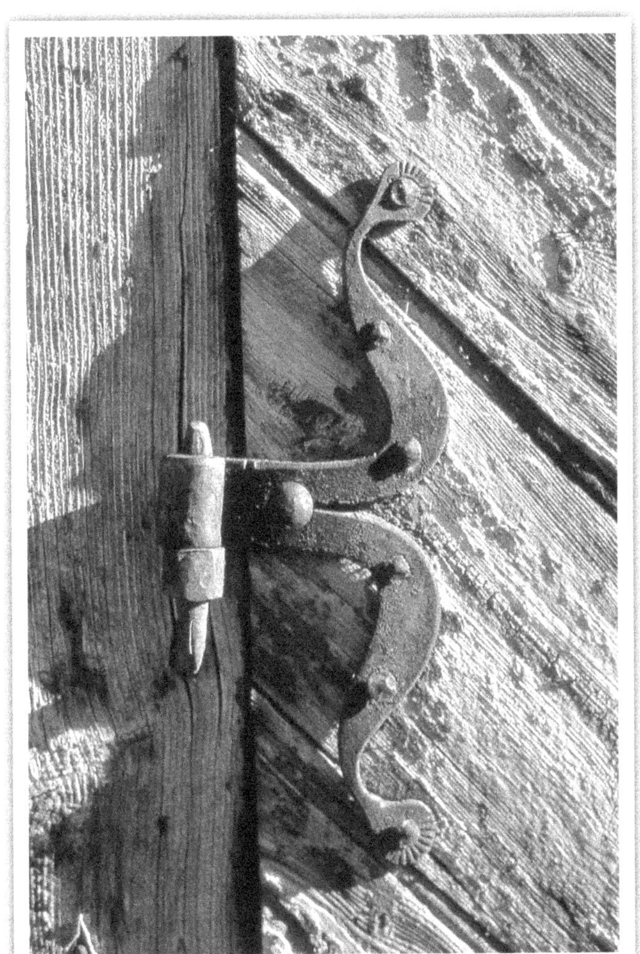

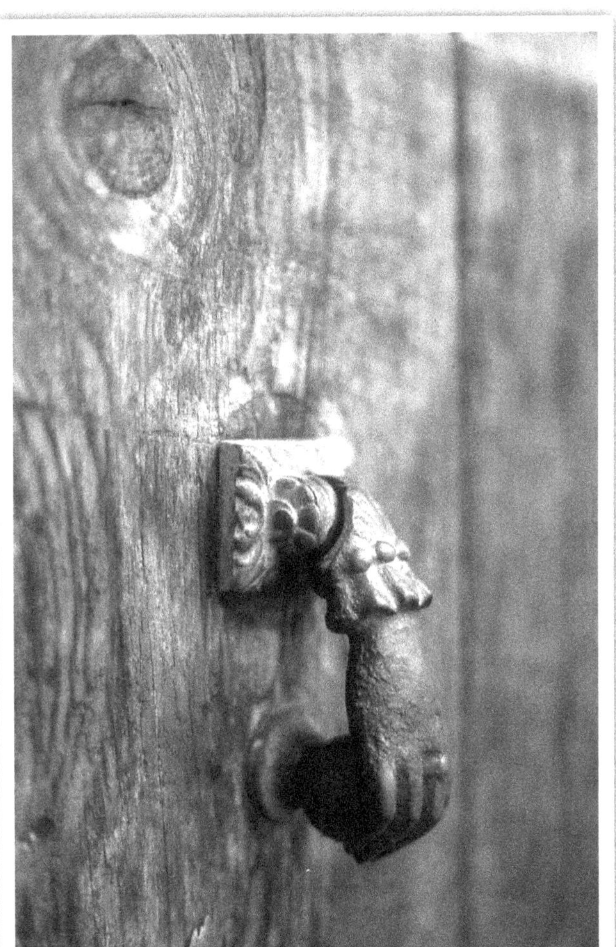

Lanuza, Province of Huesca, Aragón

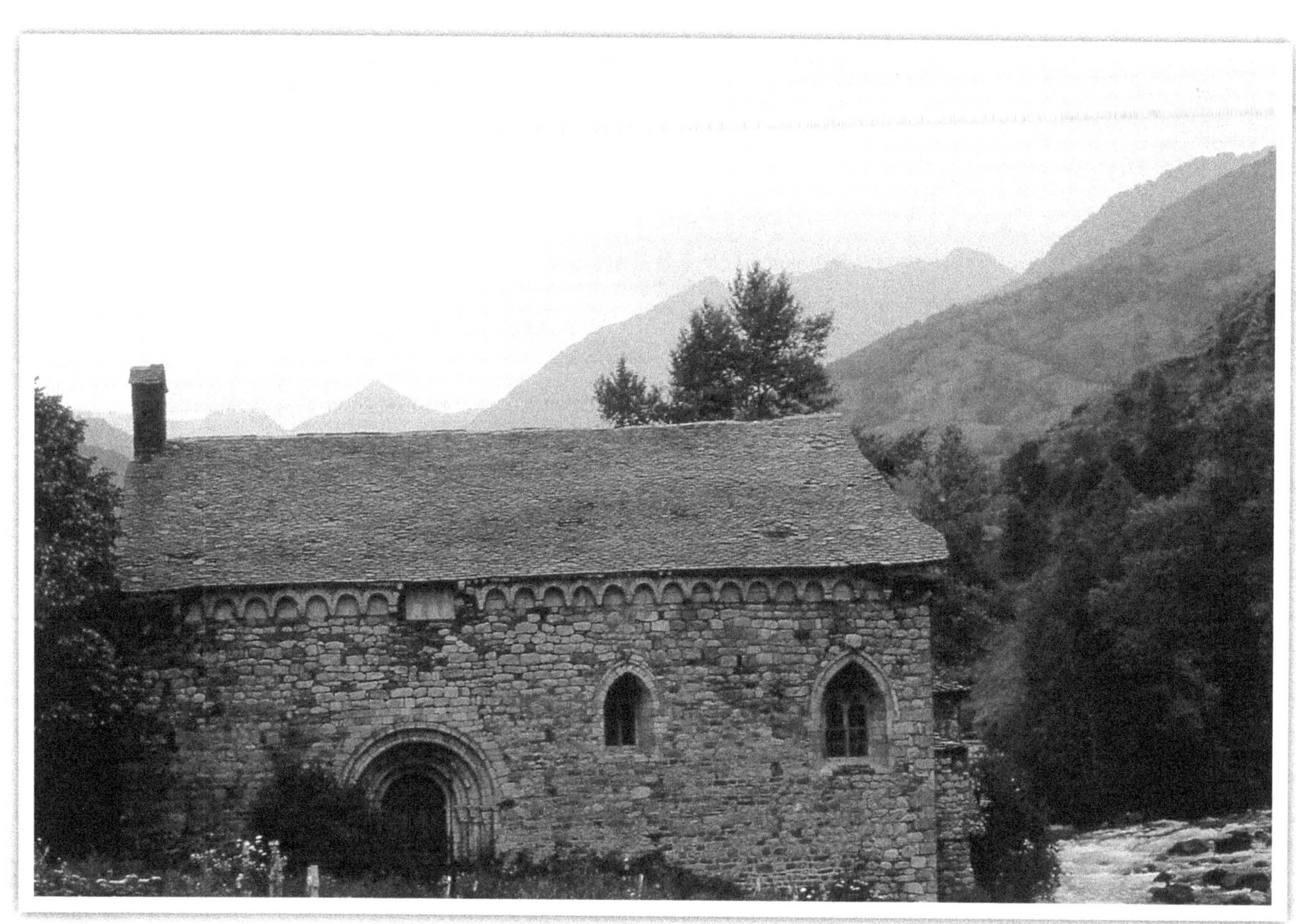

Above Viella, Province of Huesca, Aragón

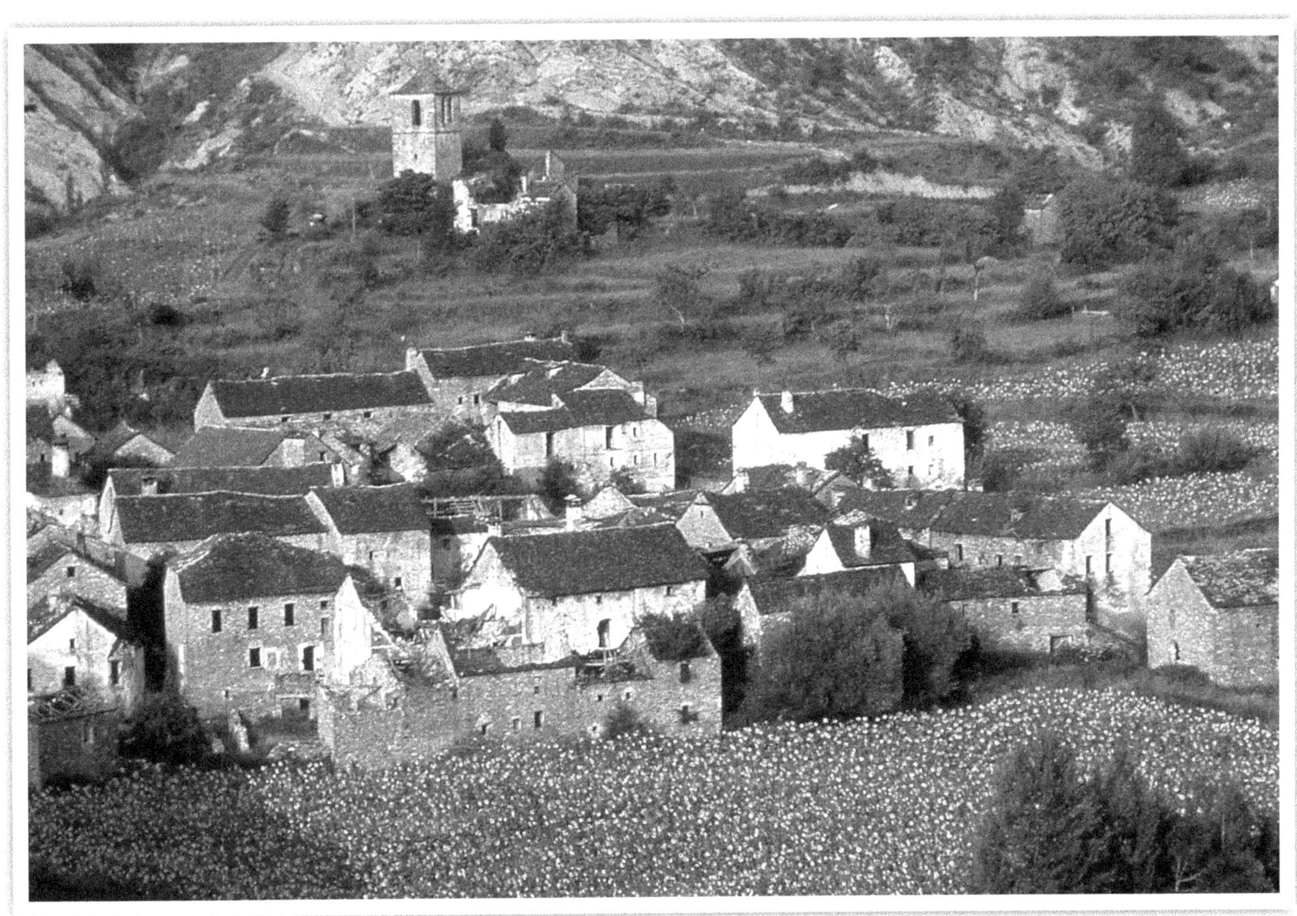

Deserted village near Lanuza

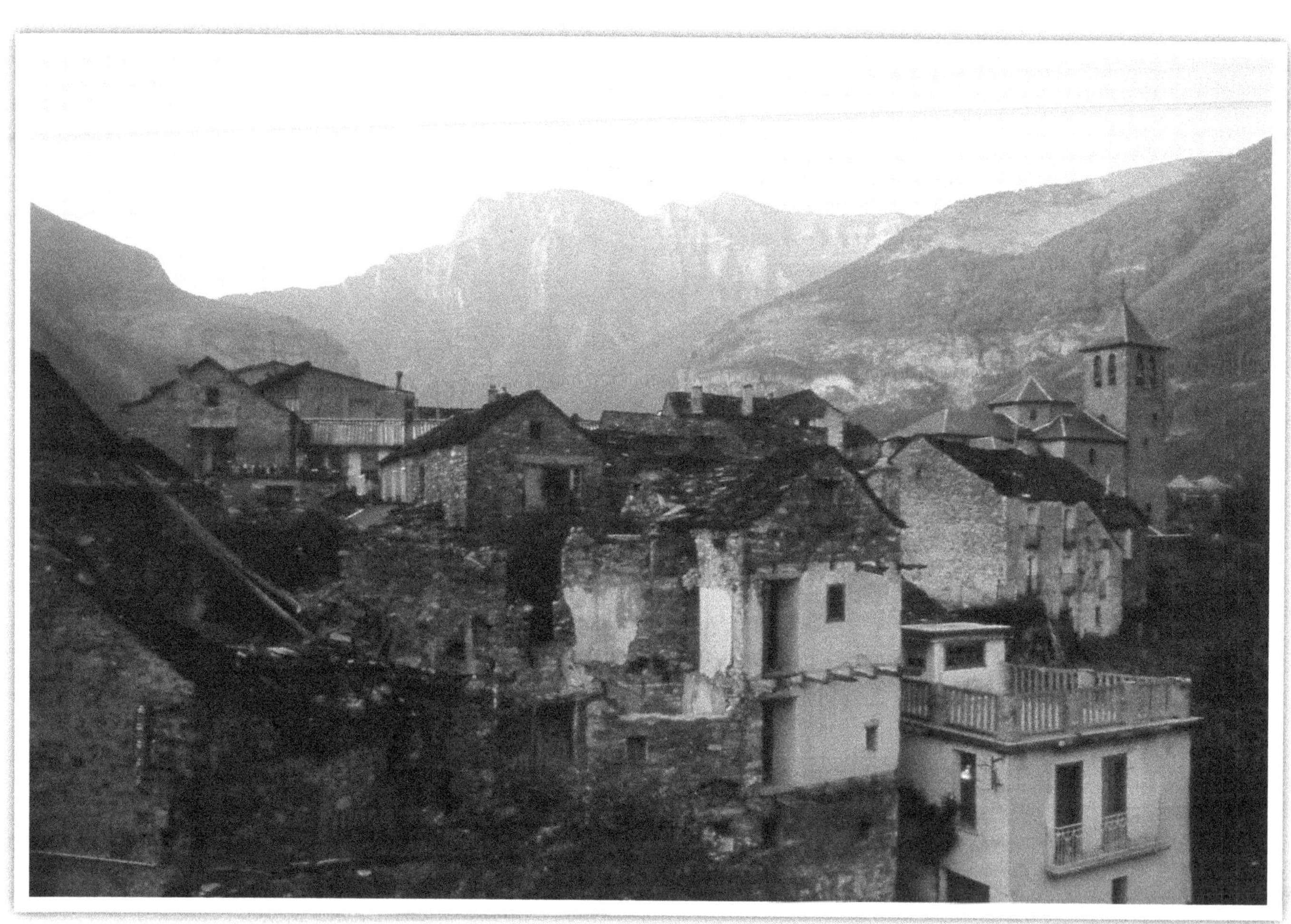

Torla/Ordesa National Park, Province of Huesca, Aragón

Places and Faces

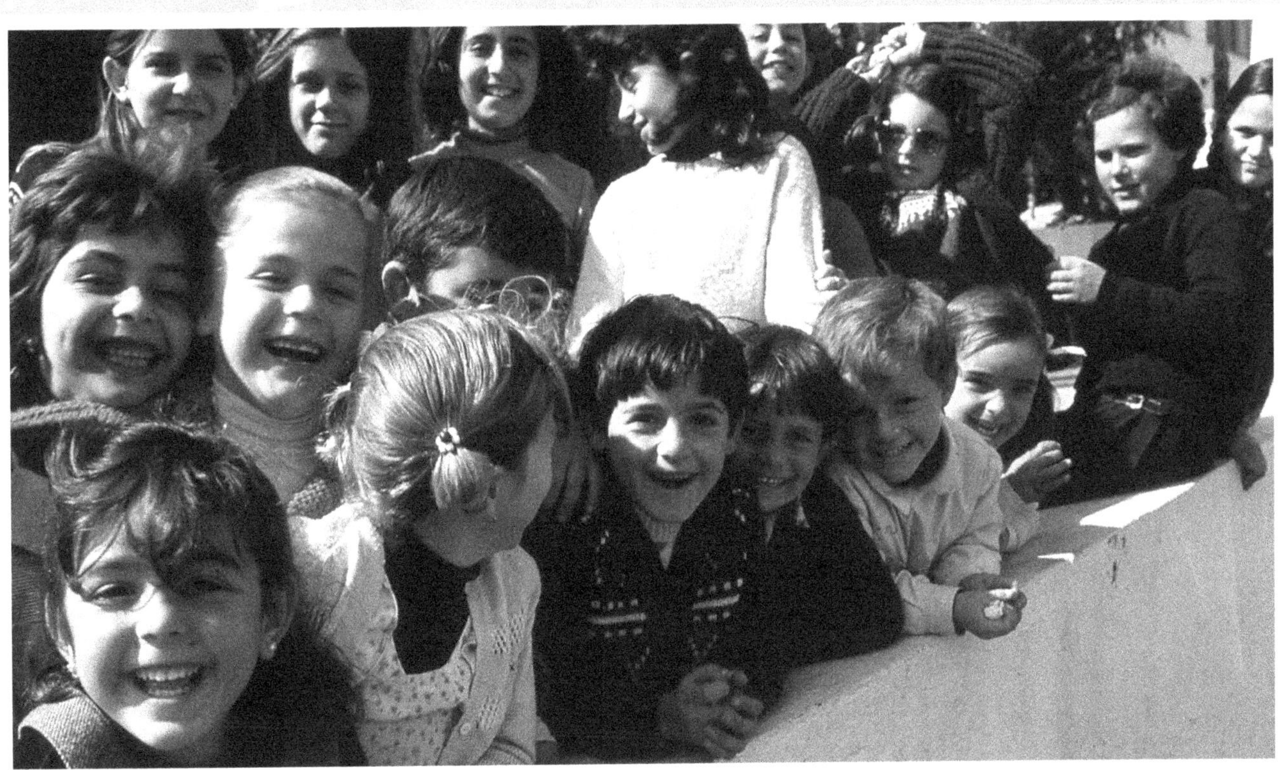

A Day in Southern Spain

Retreating from the battle lost to the rain,
the mountain spills red, rushes clay-thick
into the green, innocent sea.

After waiting out the haze
the sun remembers words to end this silence.
Now I walk into the mountains
for yellow flowers and lily leaves,
share with moss and lichen
long, clear days,
find the hooded flower tangled in ferns.
It stuns my disbelief:
light as a butterfly,
smaller than my thumb,
swaying and bobbing on its lean, white stem.
The petal, fused to an upright tube—
a translucent membrane of purple and green,
and at its crown a striped bonnet shading
the tiny threads of life.

Under a glass: a thin tongue arches
over the lip of the flower;
and within, giants stalk
in a forest of dusky trees.

A long white cloud with a flapping tail and
several fins
has fishing rights to everything in view
from this shore of the Mediterranean.
It balances on the horizon and
at nightfall is eaten,
its bones thrown to the stars.

Daydreaming of Granada and the Alhambra after Reading a Guidebook

for Ibn Zamrak, poet to the court of Mohammed V

The snow is too deep for goats.
They kick at it, making small storms
to get out, get down from the mountain.
At nightfall their stiff legs wobble and tense
as they sink to their bellies
into a harness of cold.

The palace glows pink, then red,
swelling in the late afternoon
against the distant avalanche of white.

Ibn Zamrak is inside, writing rooms of words,
tooling walls of sibilants in corridors of time,
an alphabet to praise the sultan,
Allah, snow and almond blossoms.
His indiscriminate joy is broken by arches,
sky, trees, clouds, then night and stars.

Hundred of columns,
lithe as reeds,
double in moonlight,
casting black lines over the garden of love.
Baths smelling of myrtle and pine,
avenues of pillows—
a sultan tosses an apple in the room of beds
to signal the pick of the harem—
while Andromeda chases Perseus
through the hot Andalusian sky.

His neighbors preen and
yawn in the languid night
while Zamrak lies sleepless,
worrying about the fickle court,
a sick child, and the Christians,
a cold draft from the north.

Spanish Village Remembered

In the early morning
the village, high on its citadel:
geometry of white and blue,
puzzle of sharply cut pieces
ready to explode and topple from sleep.

By midday
a hill of clover quivering
in the languid light.

I sleep and dream of my days there:
the white-haired bread man
with his shy-eyed burro,
climbing the cobbled paths;
the old women hunched in doorways,
snipping pole beans and calling to children
forever at play;
and the sea, rippled with purple at dusk, listless,
undulating, breaking, unfolding onto the sand.

I've enough for this infatuation:
photos, a relief map,
delicate swirls tightening up from the coast
to distant fields of snow.
Books of pressed flowers.
A place off season, out of time, secure.

Spanish Generalizations

All Spaniards love canaries.
Cages of singing birds dot walls in houses and hotels,
sharing a beatific vision with the weeping virgin
and suffering saints.
Untroubled in this paradise, the birds proclaim
a litany of faith:
"We like it here and do renounce
and are content and do believe."

In the family bar
hams hang near painted plates,
blood sausages, Fanta and Coke signs,
more canaries, the Sacred Heart of Jesus,
and a blaring T.V.
Everyone shouts, unless sick or sad, and all the men
have short legs
and are proud of their young, tall daughters, so pretty
in their long American jeans.

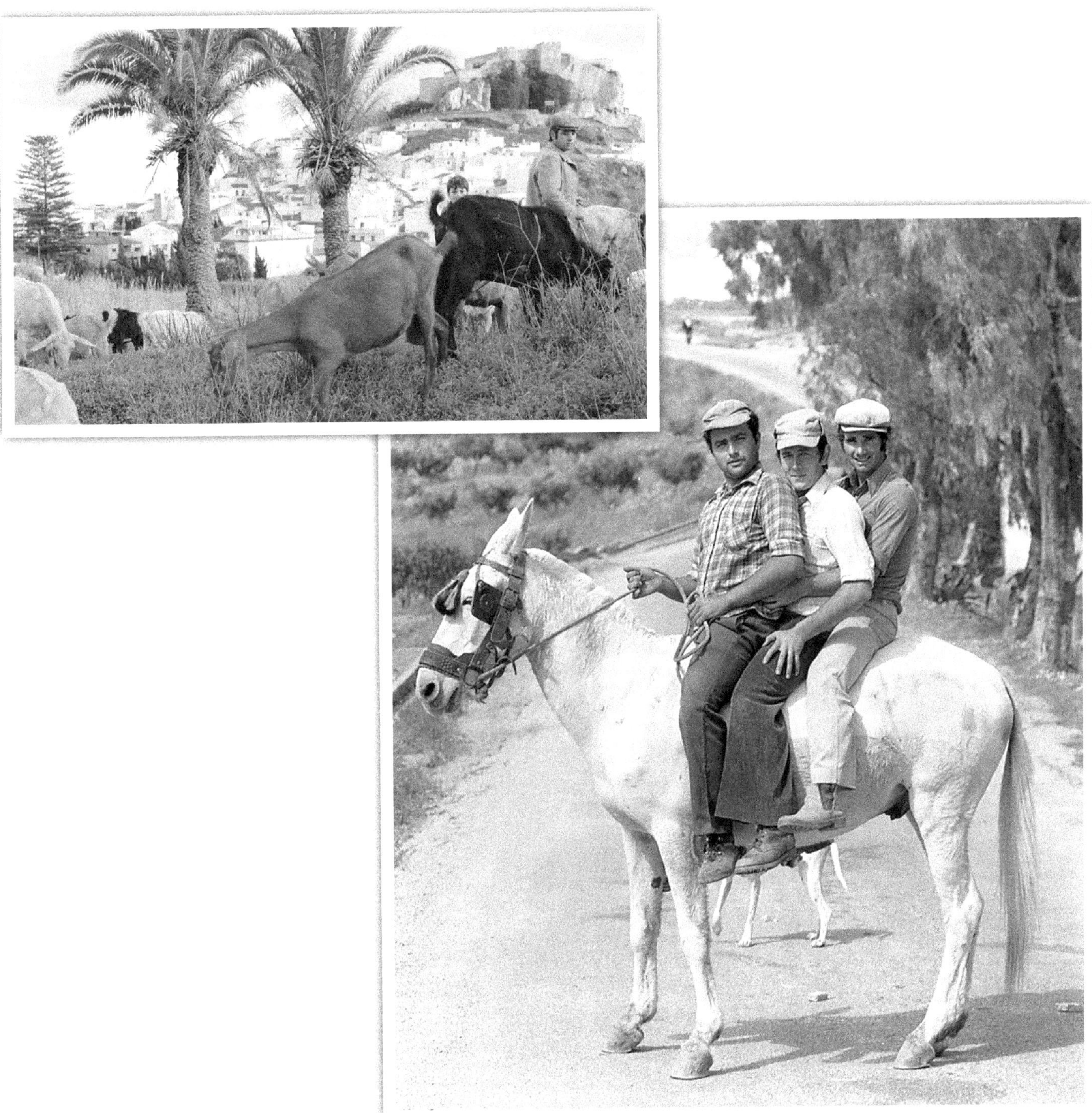

Salobreña, Province of Granada, Andalusia

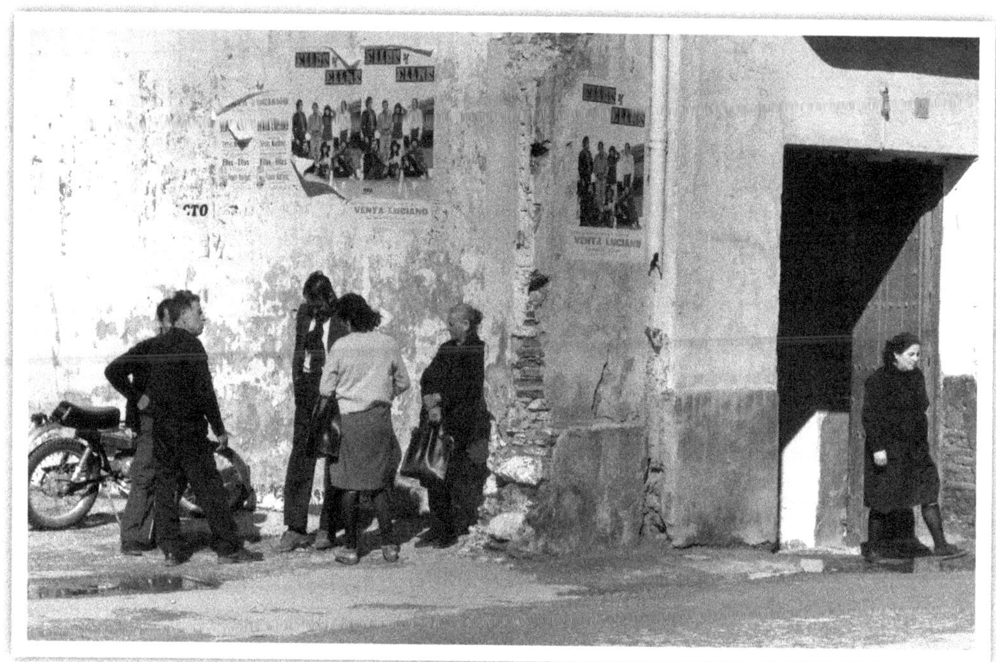

Almuñecar, Province of Granada, Andalusia

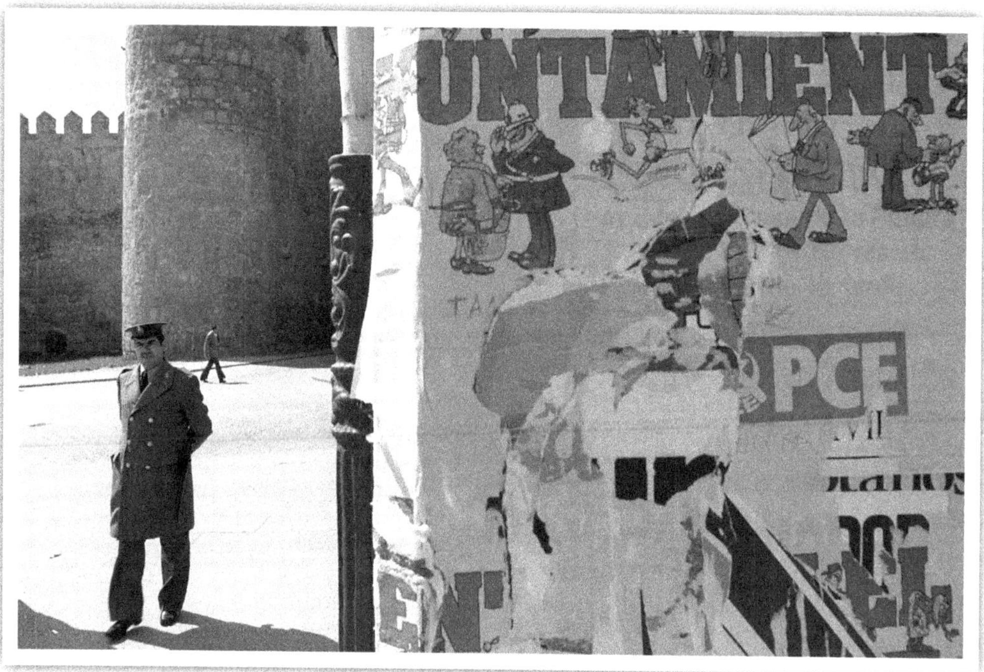

Ávila, Province of Ávila, Castilla y León

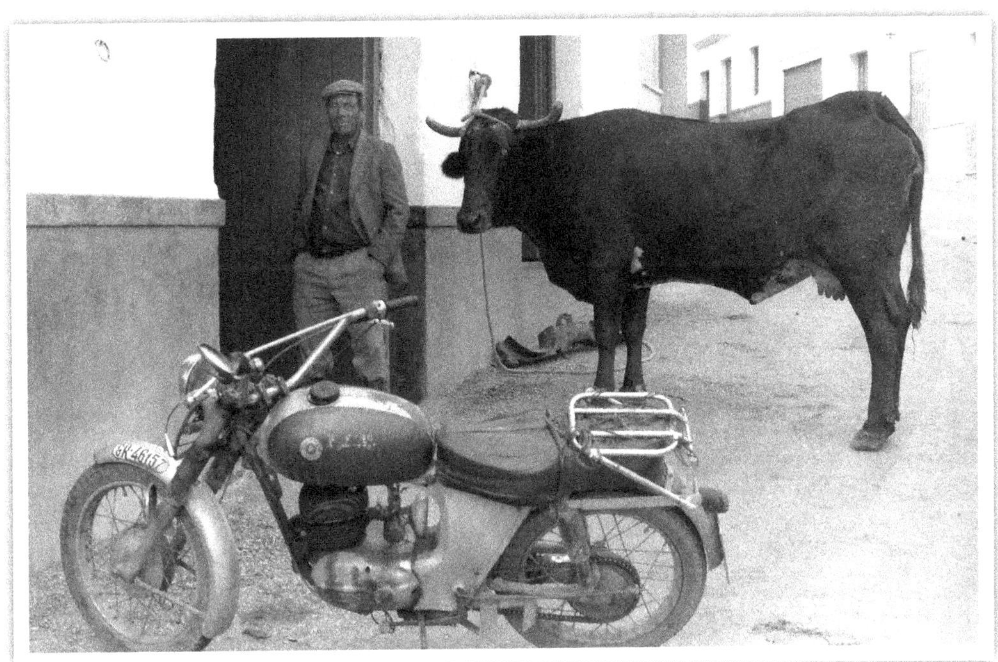

Man, cow, and Bultaco bike, Salobreña

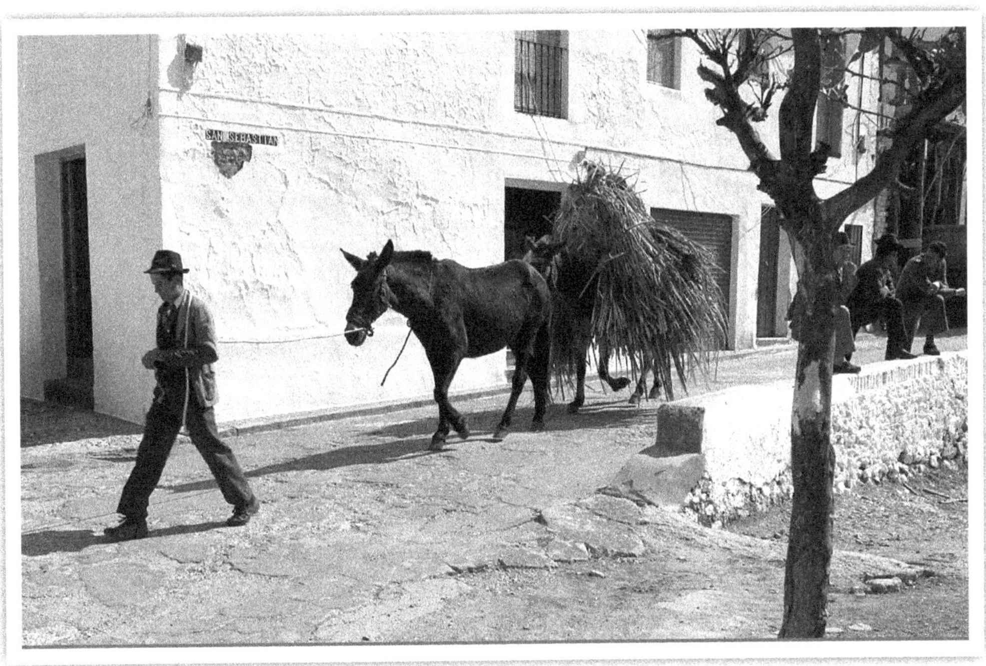

Frigiliana, Province of Málaga, Andalusia

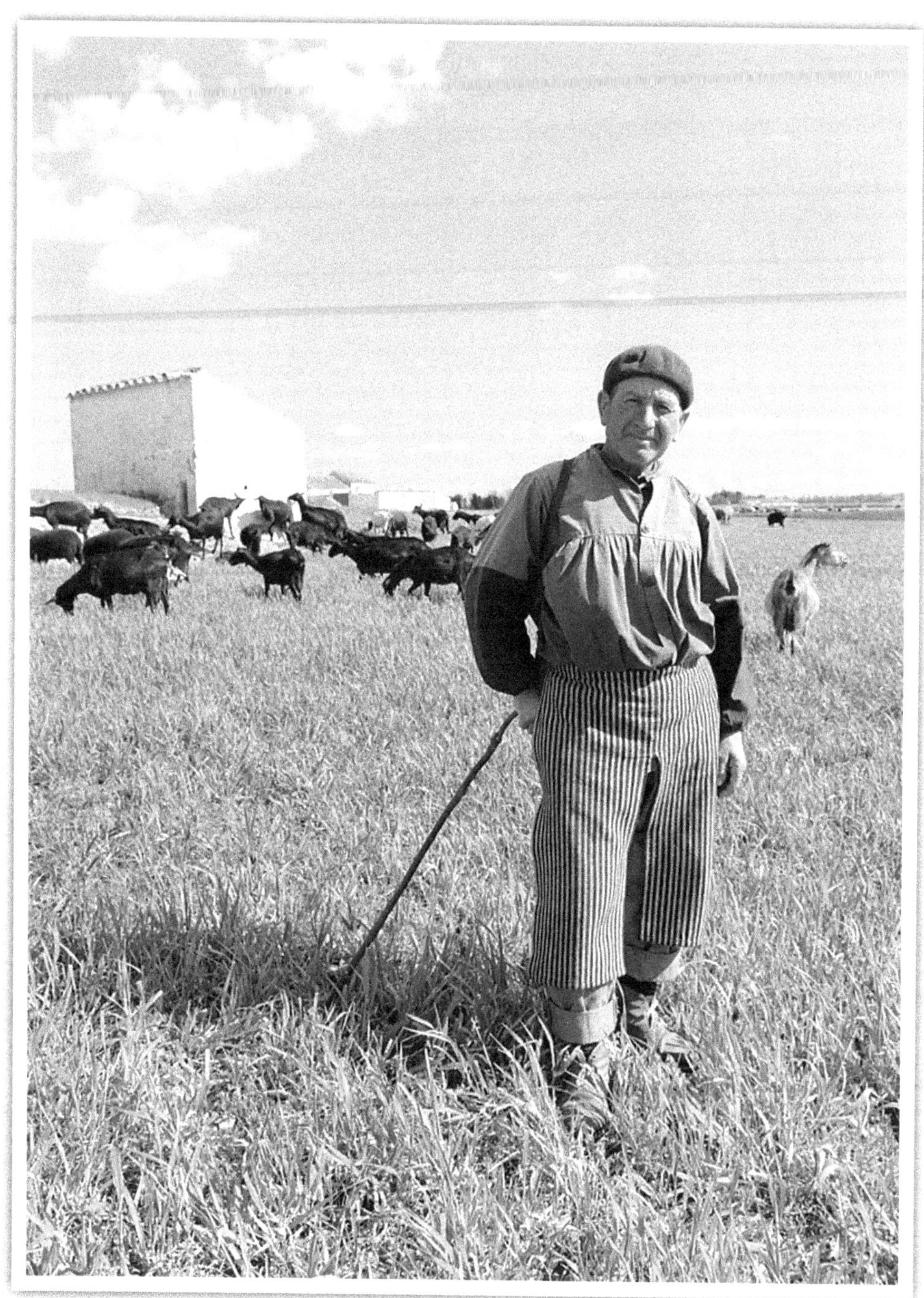

Near Consuegra, Province of Toledo, Castilla-La Mancha

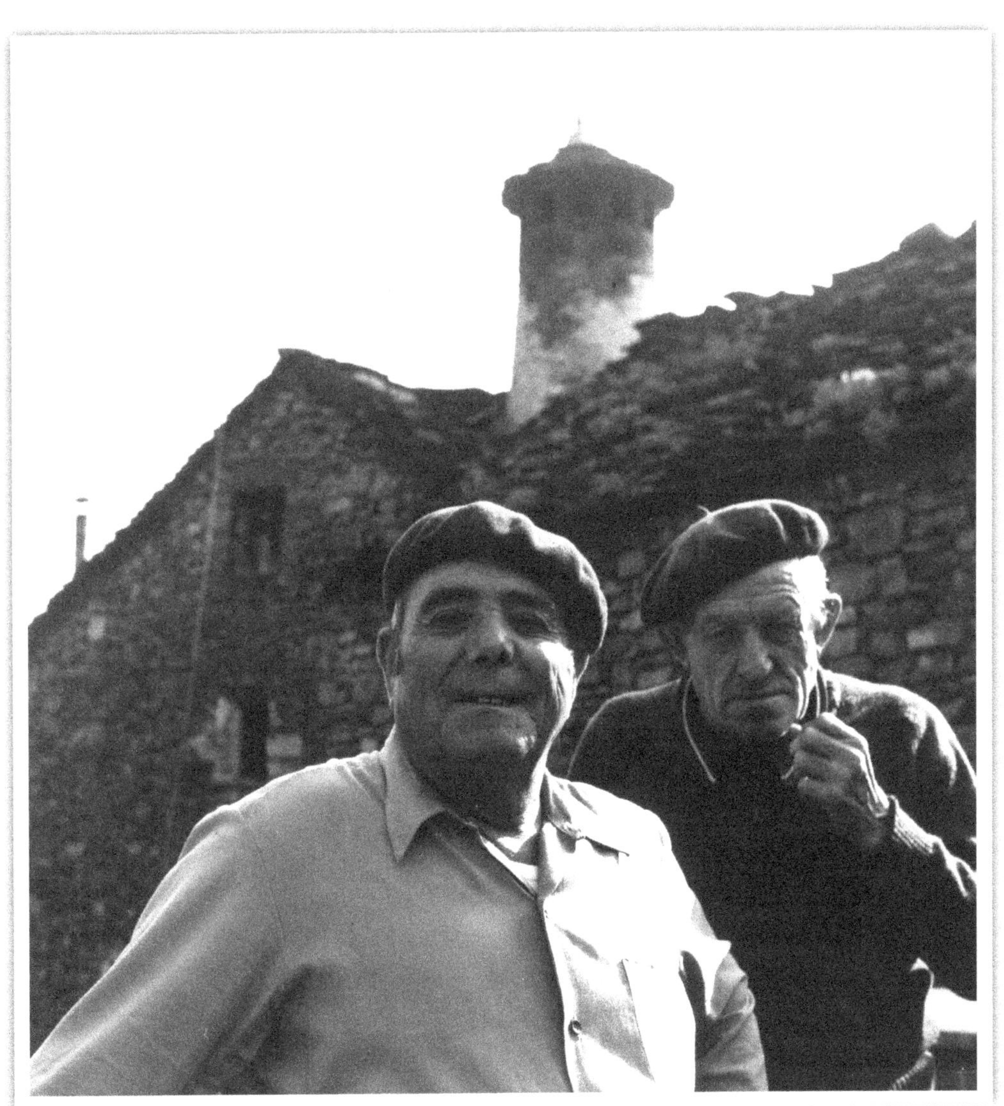

Boinas españolas, Castilla-La Mancha

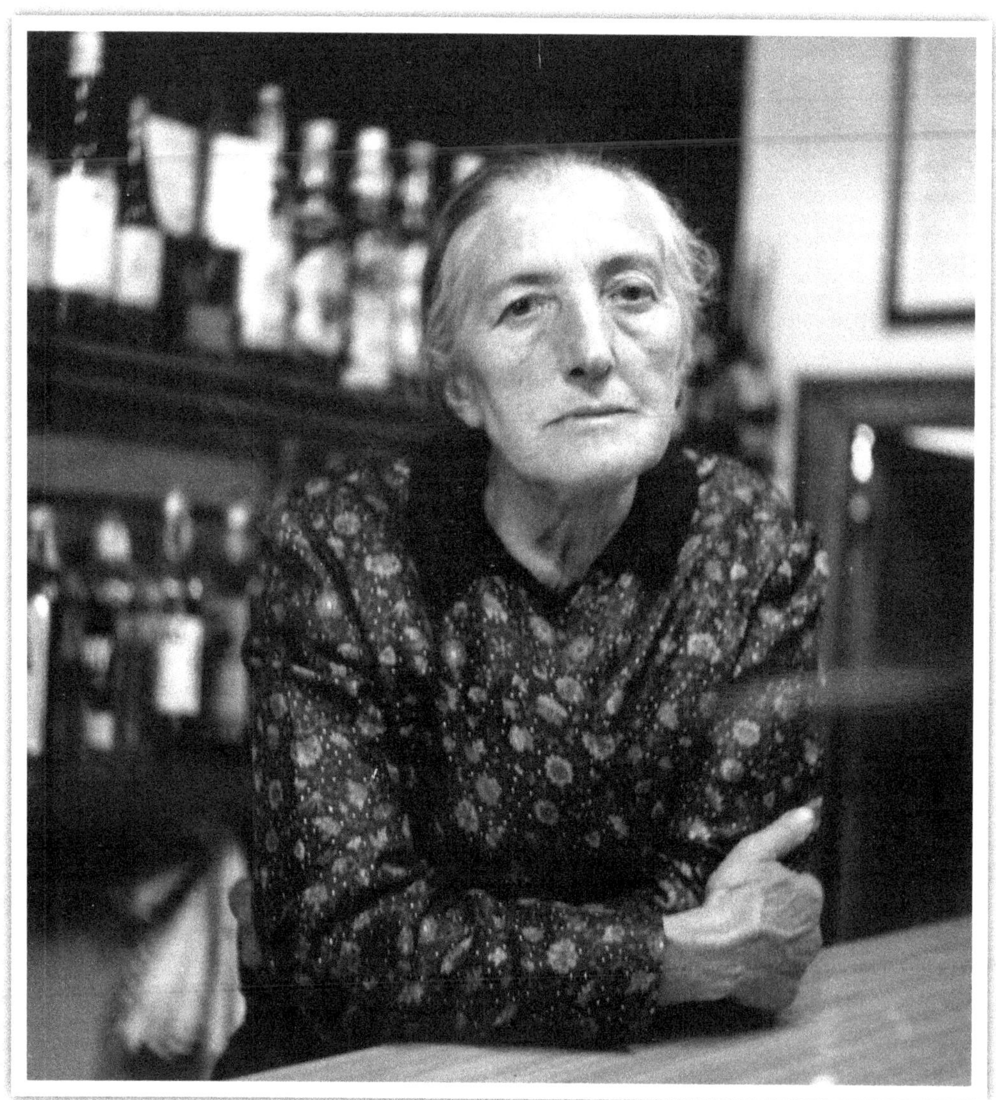

Bar owner, Portilla de la Reina, Province of León, Castilla y León

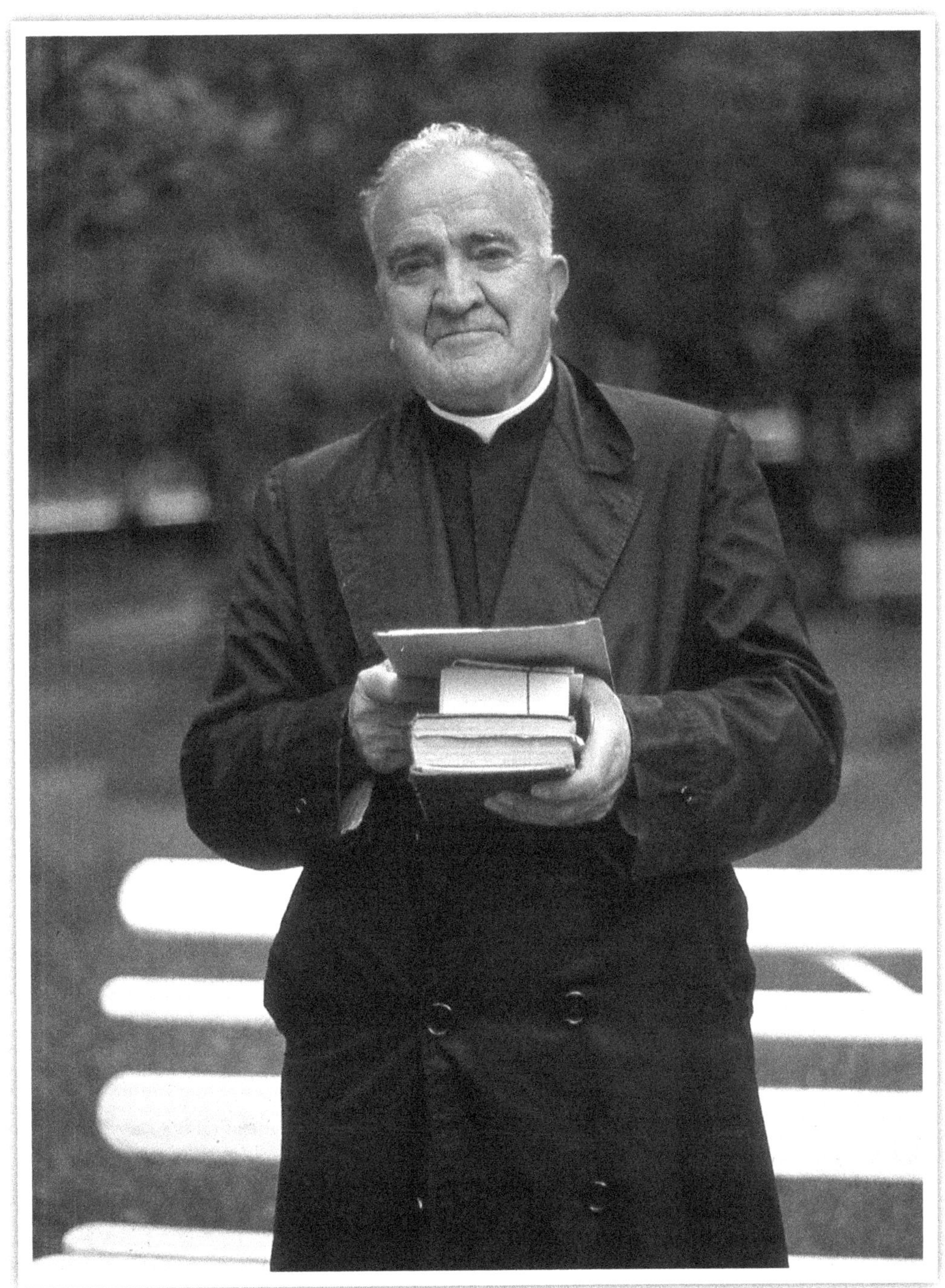

Padre, Balneario de Panticosa, Huesca Province, Aragón

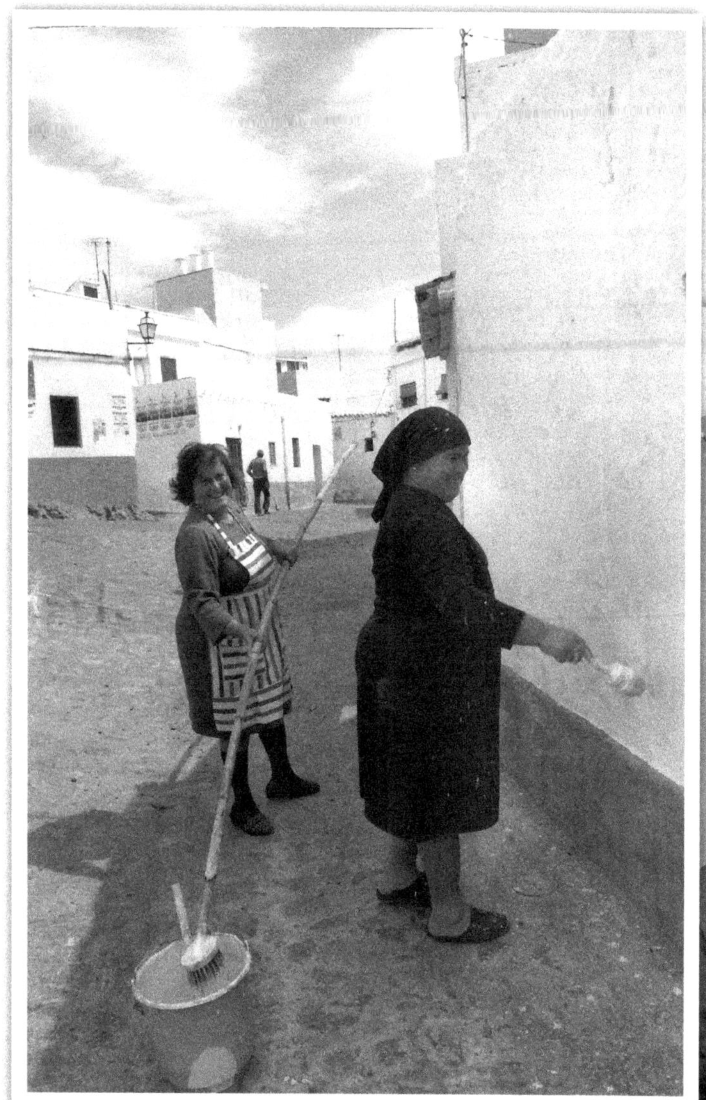

Sisters, spring whitewashing, Almuñecar

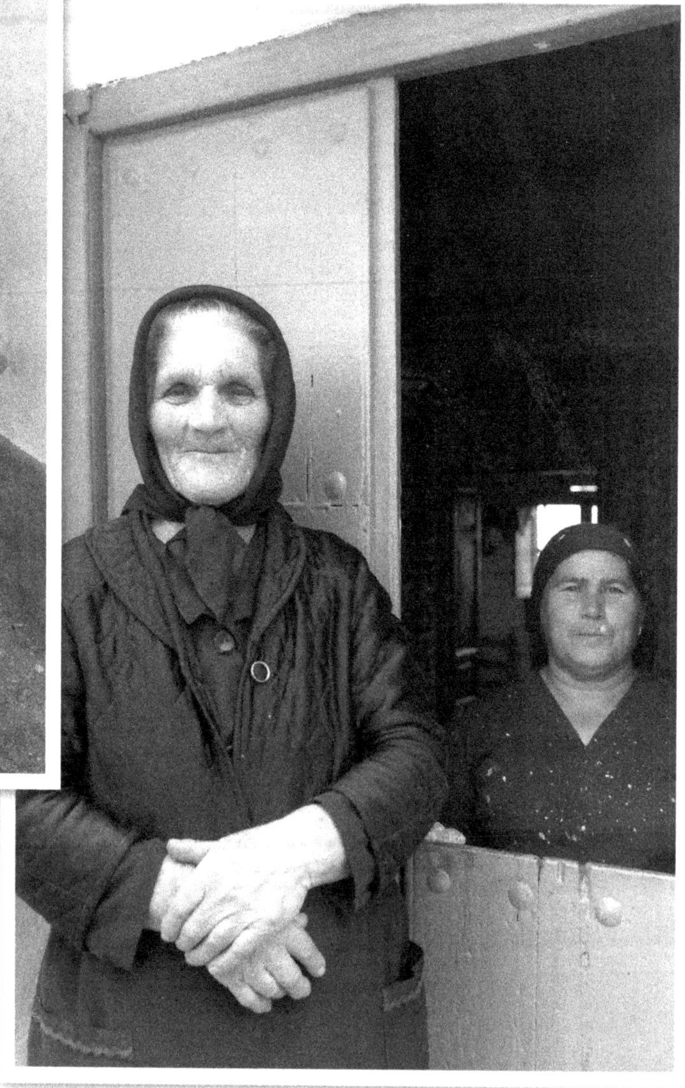

Mother and daughter, Almuñecar

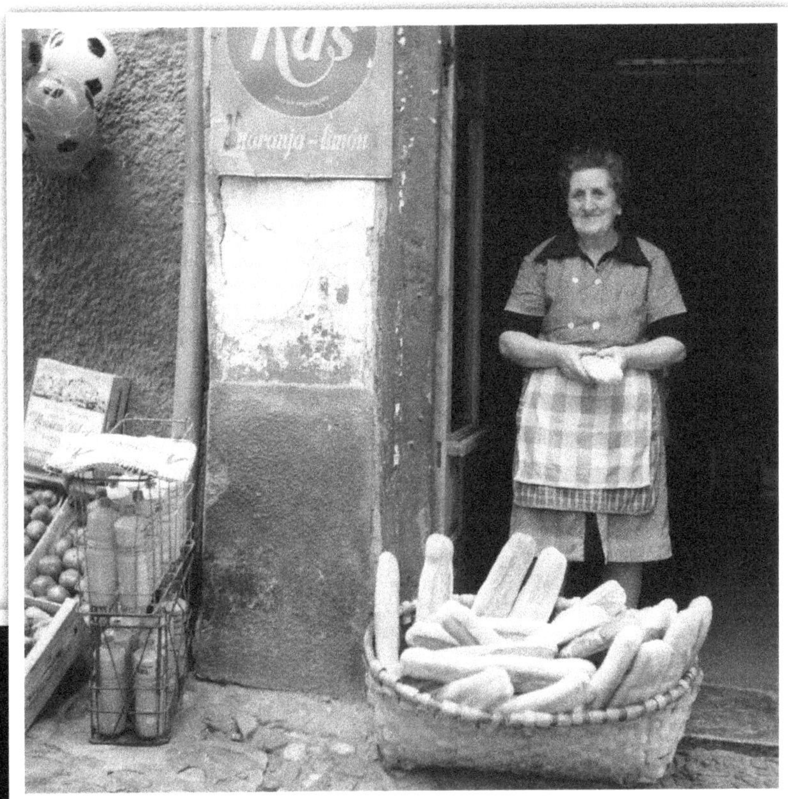

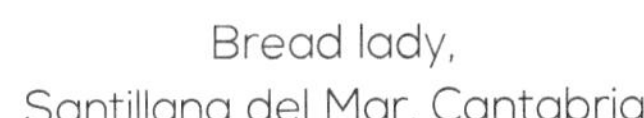

Bread lady,
Santillana del Mar, Cantabria

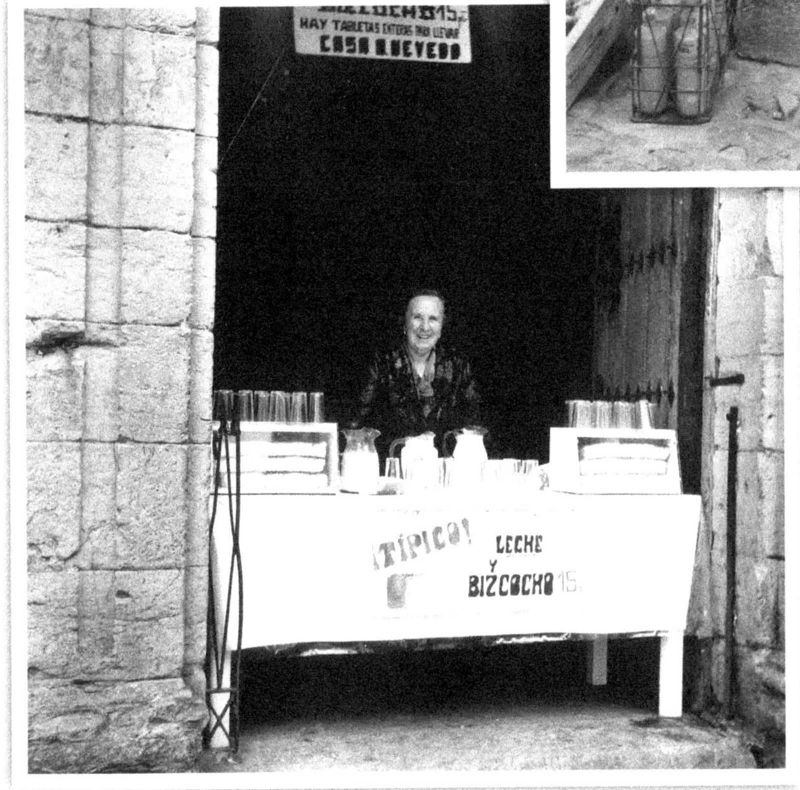

Milk lady, Santillana del Mar, Cantabria

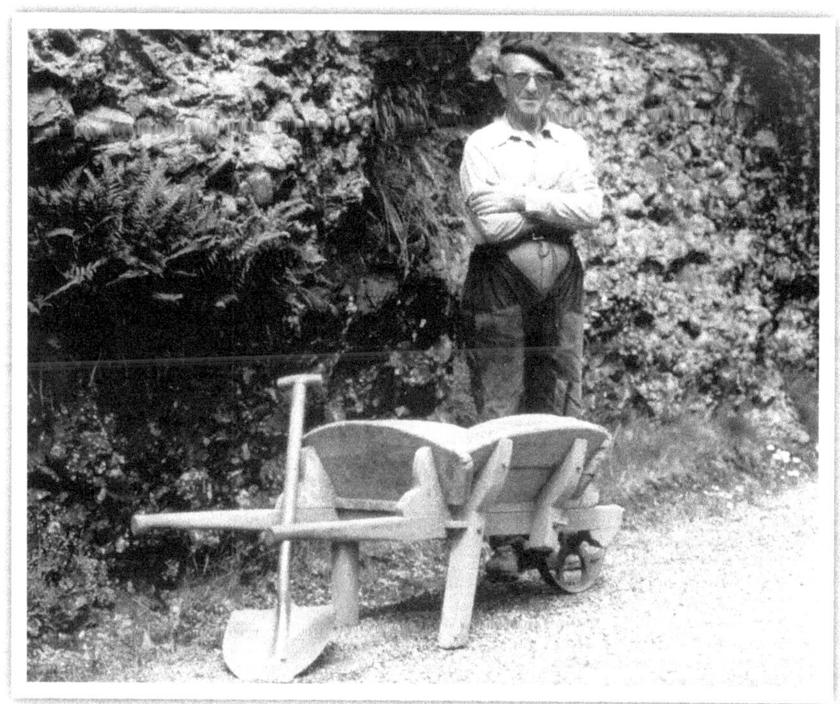

"Roadmender", Province of Palencia, Castilla y León

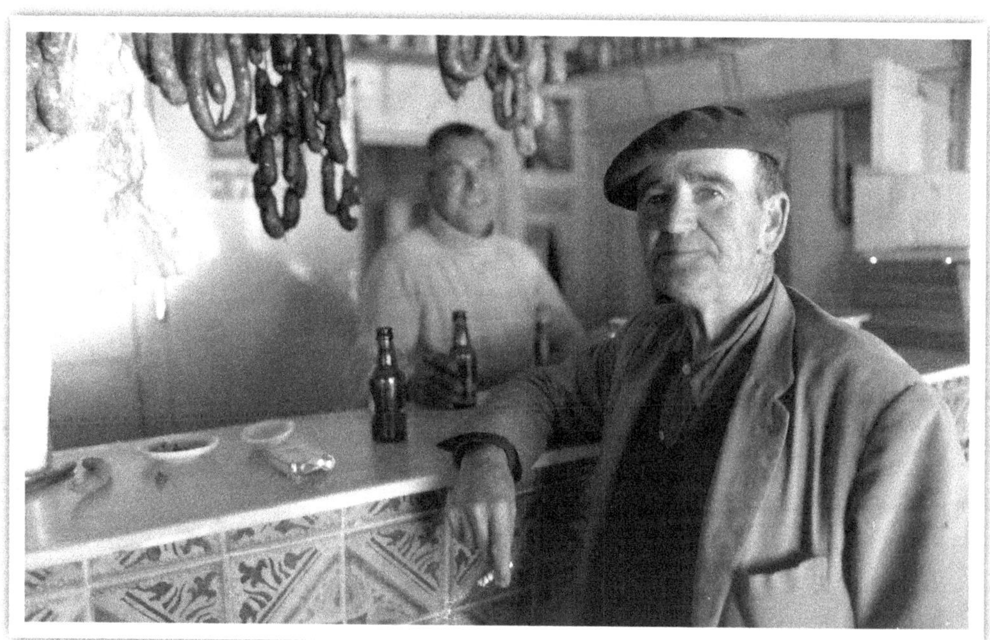

Otivar, Province of Granada, Andalusia

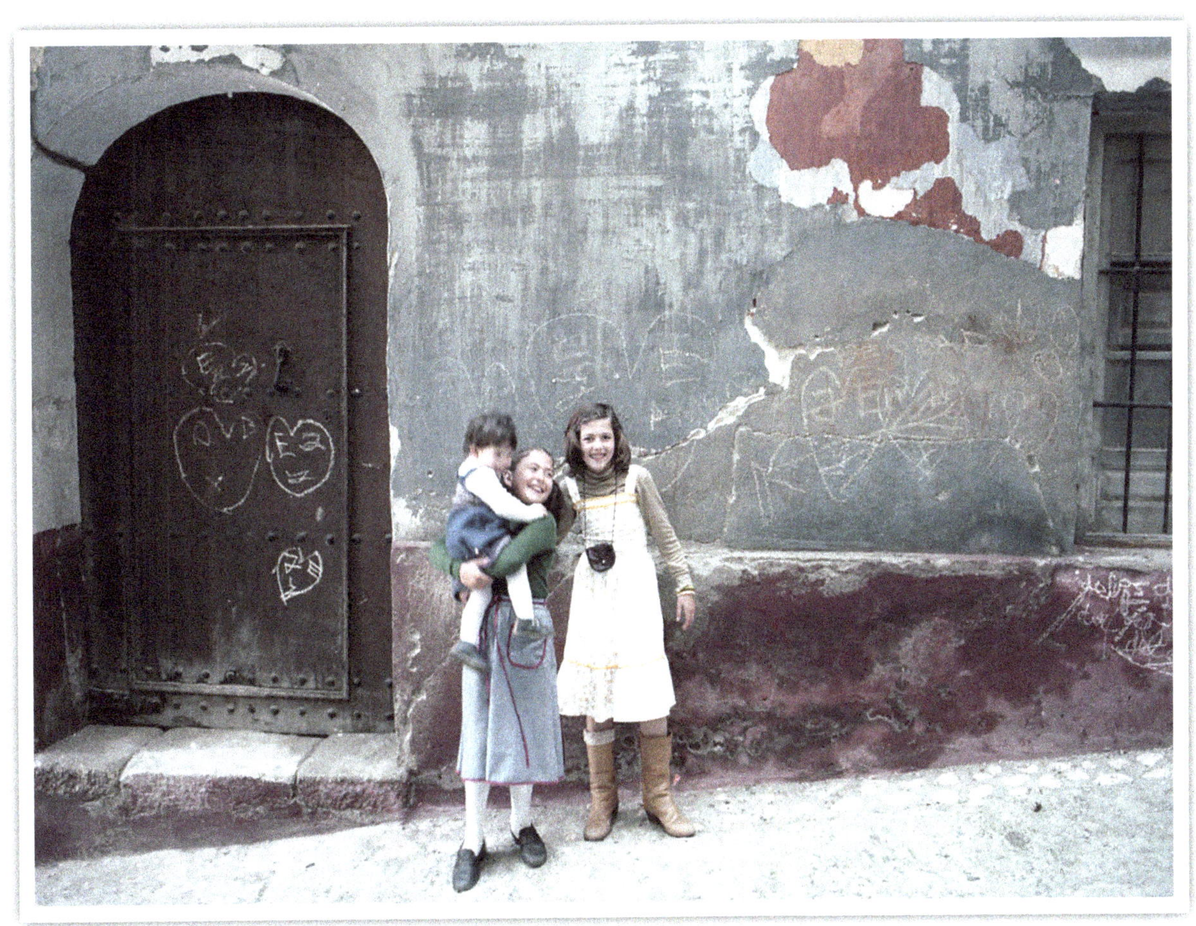

Almuñecar, Province of Granada, Andalusia

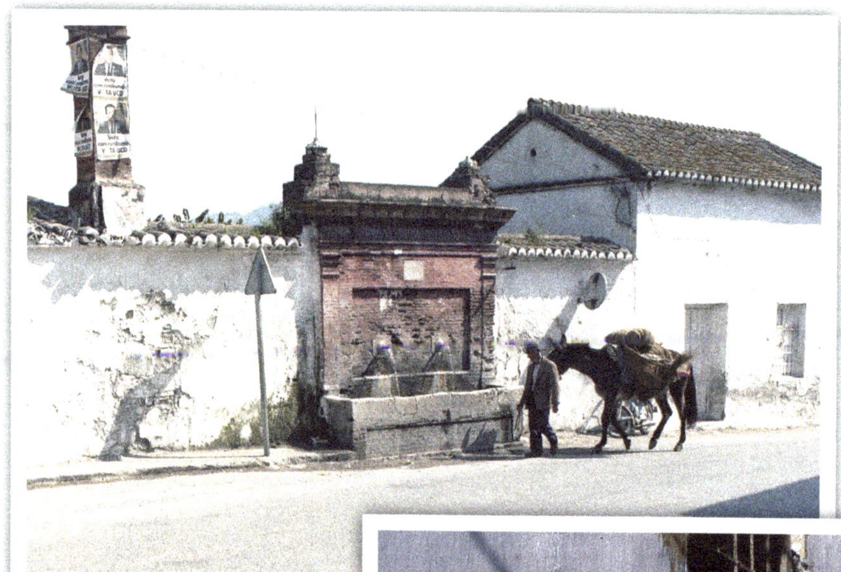

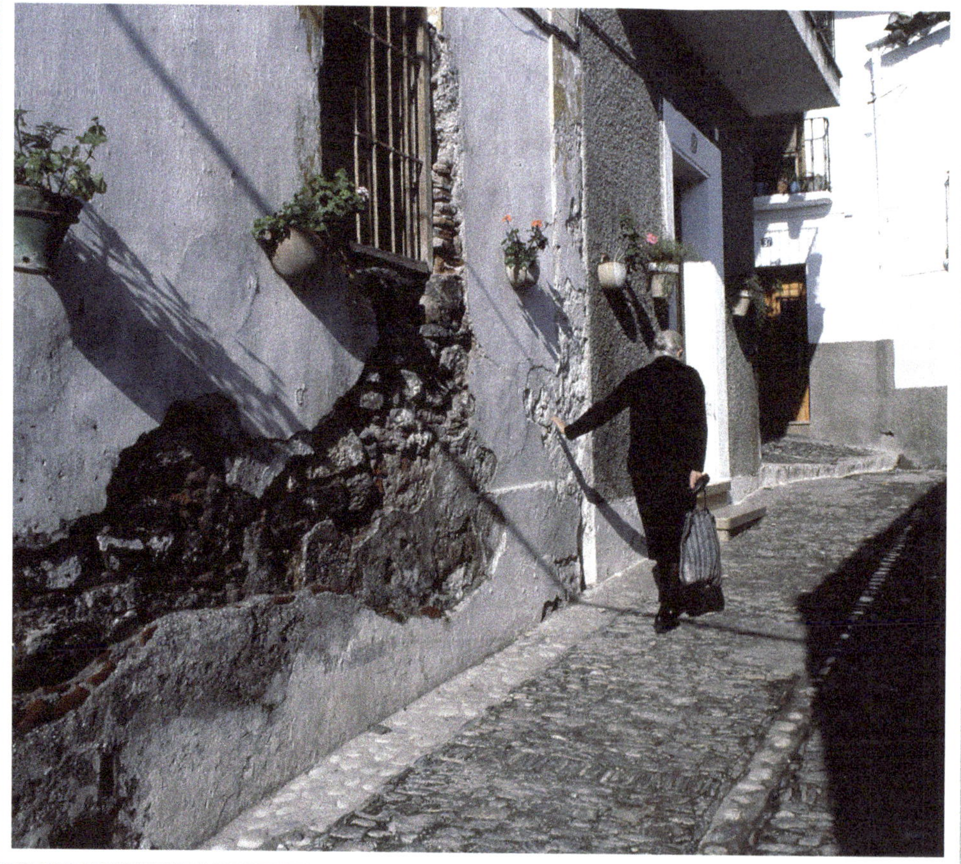

Almuñecar street scenes

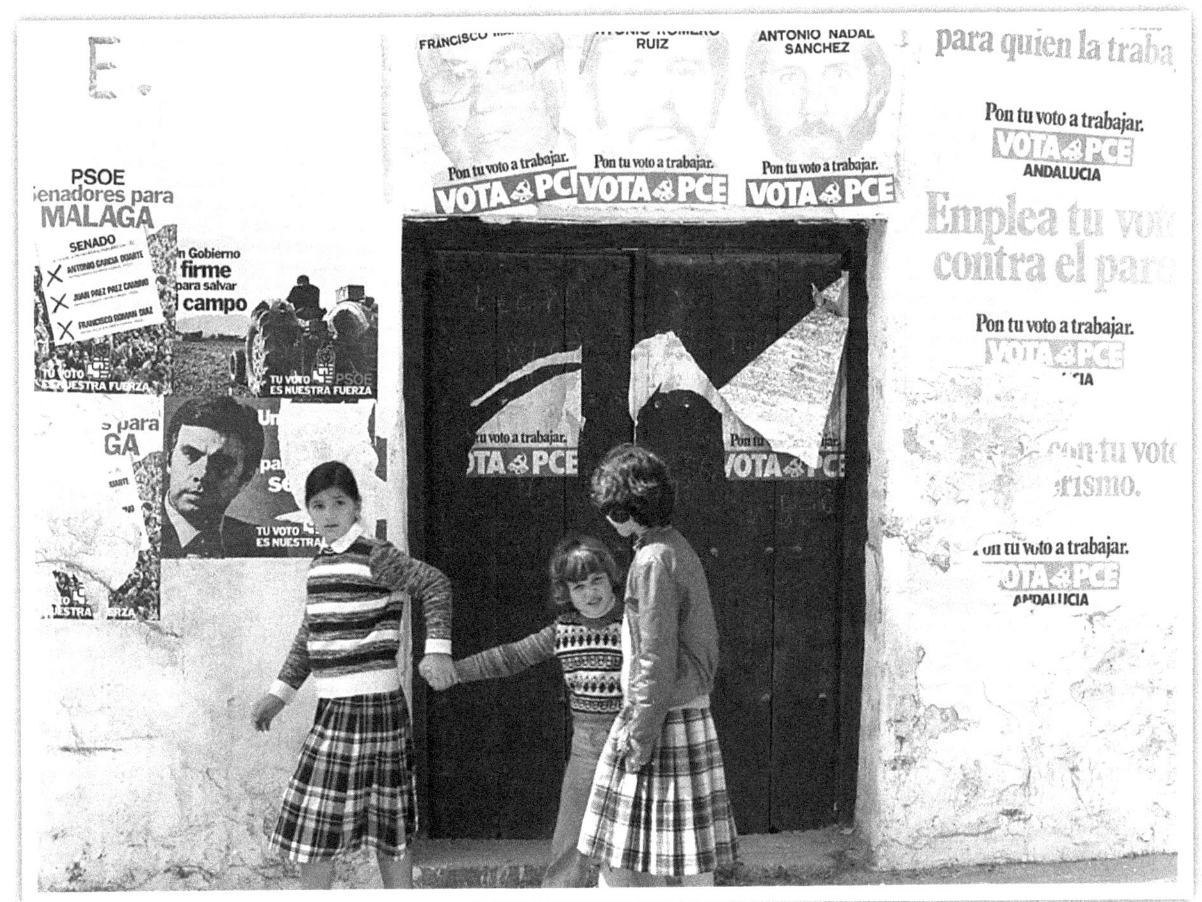

Nerja, Province of Granada, Andalusia

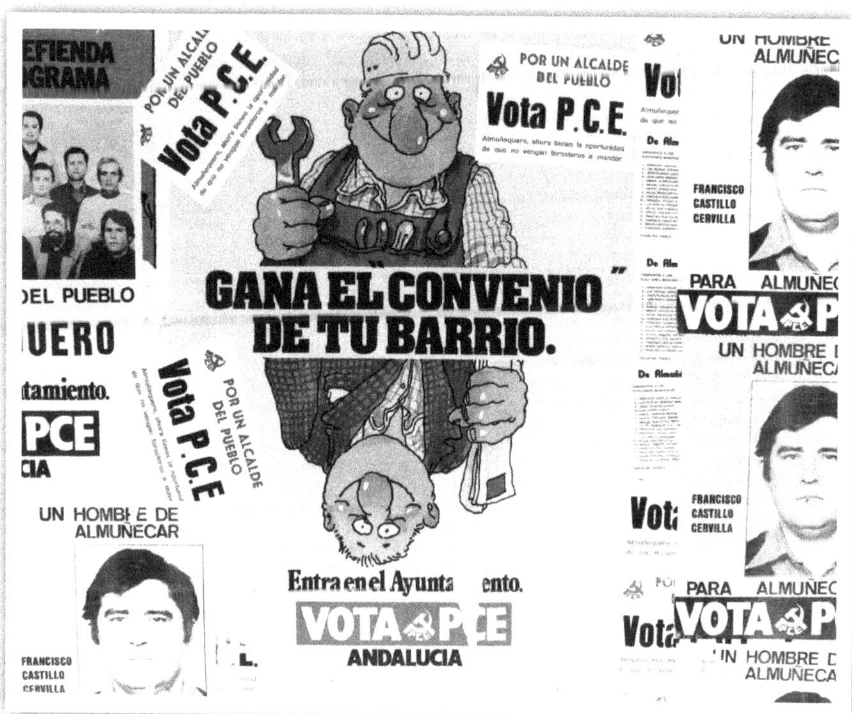

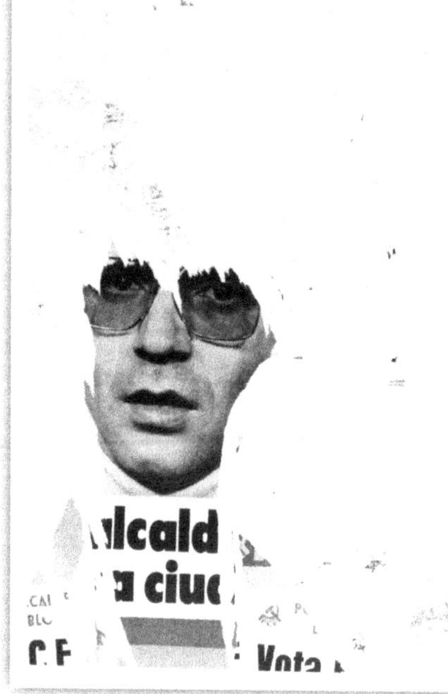

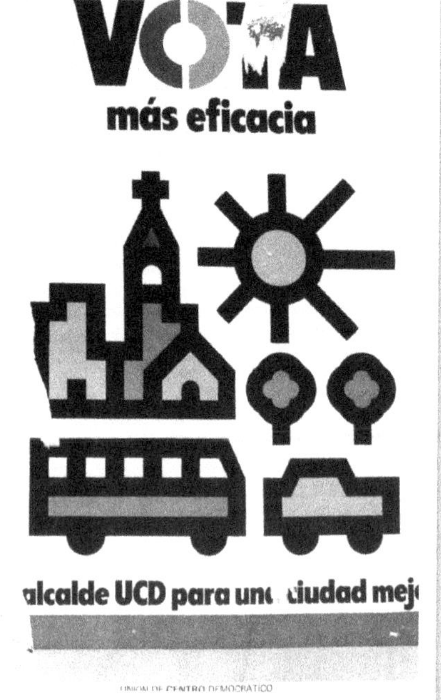

Political posters, Almuñecar

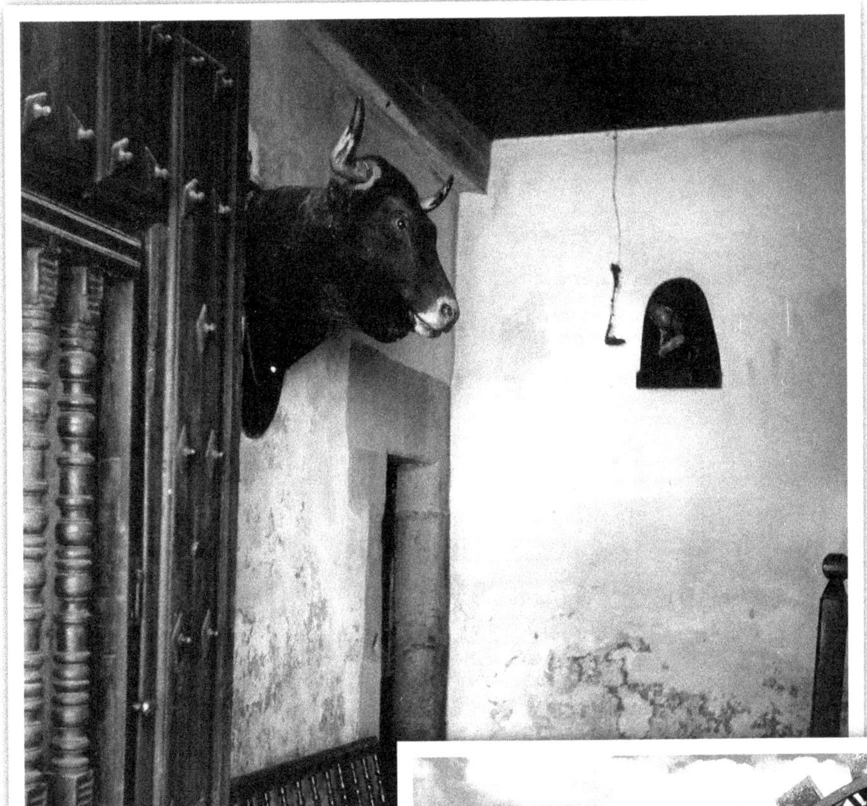

Almuñecar

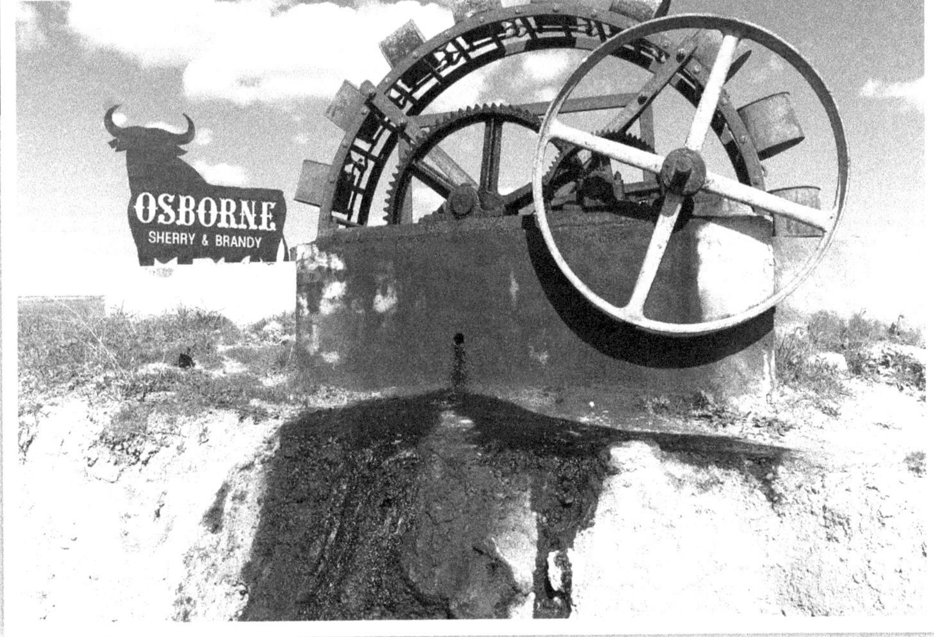

Near Consuegra, Province of Toledo, Castilla-La Mancha

The Sea Is a Good Mother to Cats

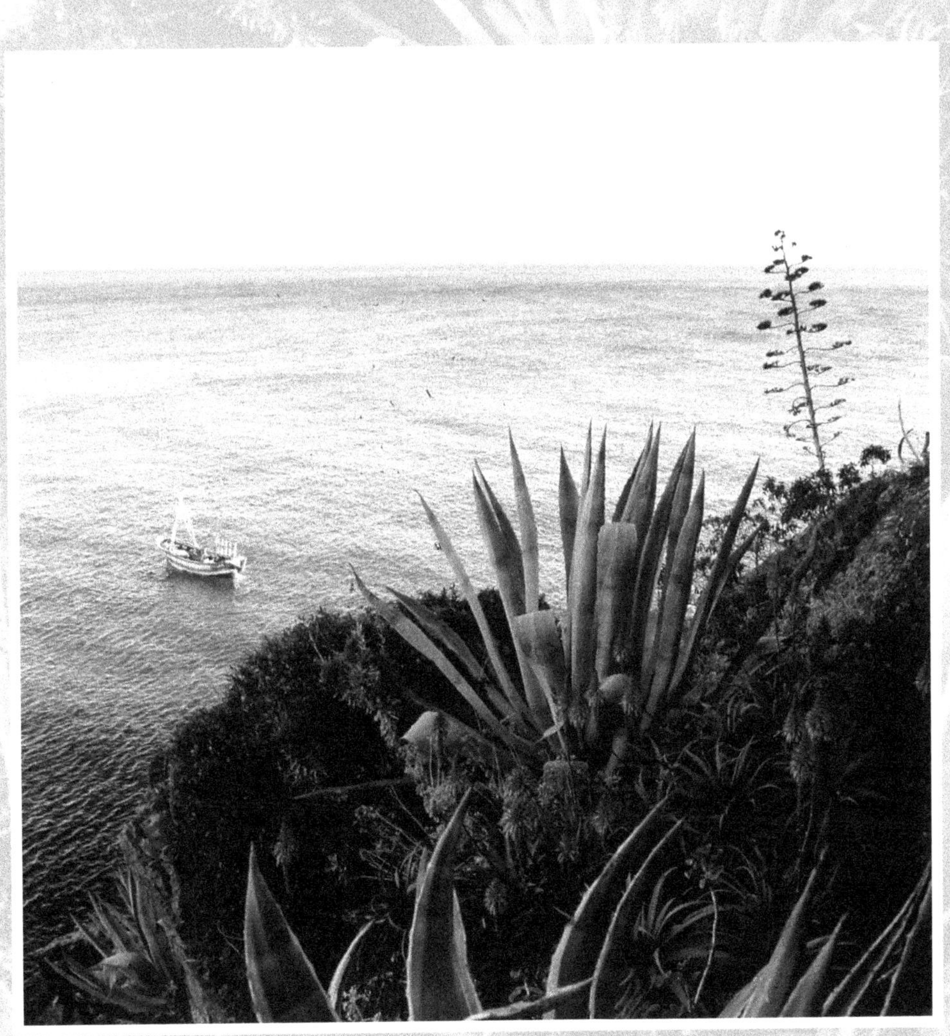

The Sea

The sea is a good mother to cats.
They roll and stretch on the pebble beach,
watching the water toss up broken pieces:
fish heads, bits of mussels,
tiny crab legs—a mine of soft, salty meat—
plastic bottles, rotting timbers,
now and then a dying bird
shivering above the perpetual tumble.

They are at home,
this family of good, fast feet and
sleek indifference—
their fearless noses poking in sand for snails
the fishermen leave for the beach wino.

He throws stones at them, curses, coughs,
builds a little junk fire for the snails.
Fat enough for patience

but the cats can't wait for a feast.
They paw at the fire
while the wino curls closer to the warmth,
sliding in and out of sleep.
The snails hiss and bubble,
nearly swelling out of their charred shells.

Then he wakes, bellowing and spitting in sick, cold anger.
His shirt flapping buttonless,
he kicks the smoldering fire at the cats, at the sea—
the snails, his dinner, sailing back into the water.

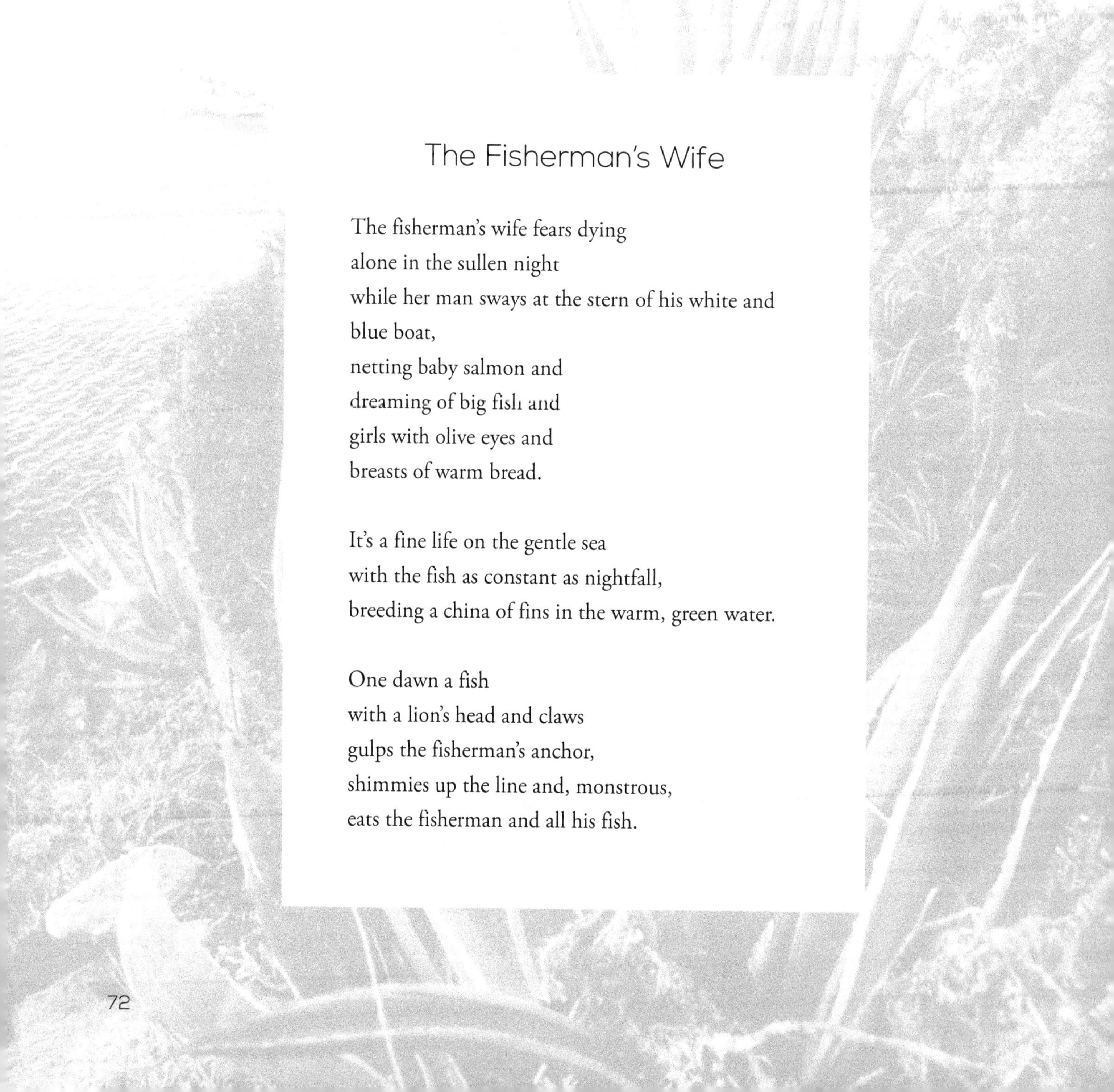

The Fisherman's Wife

The fisherman's wife fears dying
alone in the sullen night
while her man sways at the stern of his white and
blue boat,
netting baby salmon and
dreaming of big fish and
girls with olive eyes and
breasts of warm bread.

It's a fine life on the gentle sea
with the fish as constant as nightfall,
breeding a china of fins in the warm, green water.

One dawn a fish
with a lion's head and claws
gulps the fisherman's anchor,
shimmies up the line and, monstrous,
eats the fisherman and all his fish.

The little boat rocks home,
light glistening like silver scales on the sea's rolling back.

On the shore the wife waits
with bread, sausage, and slices of potato.
Her dark eyes are jealous of the wandering sea,
her voice hard and strident as she calls
to the boy chasing gulls in shallow water.

At last the boat drifts in, riding low,
nearly swallowed by the breakers,
heavy with fish, a silent man, and
a golden turtle.

Scene from My Balcony

A man in a bathrobe and shoes and socks
is lying on the pebble beach.
He's in the rectangle
I frame with my balcony railings:
there, between the green fishing boat
that never moves
and the wooden cable spool
that rolls from the pebbles and sand
into the white fingers of the sea,
and rolls until it's pushed back again
by the breakers.

Palm trees promenade,
wind turning their heads
inland toward the sighing village.

A dog is jumping for a stick
near a red car.

The man stands,
sits, seems to call the dog,
lies cockeyed with his head
sloping dangerously toward the water.
I lean to the left and my railing
takes off his head—a shocking composition.
After a few minutes I bring him back,
only to see he wants to leave.
He gets into the red car
and drives between the jumping dog
and four Brits who are bowling
with steel balls
on the long shadowed sand.

This happens three times a week
at least—
the spool, the bowling Brits,
the jumping dog and stick—
all except the man
in the sandy bathrobe.

The Discovery of a Fragment of the Sea

It is winter
in another country.

Clouds up from Africa,
warm drizzle, then glaring sun.

From my balcony I am higher than gulls.

Light and water,
a broken mirror that rides the green waves
of the Mediterranean.

Our small Gibraltar
points its snout out to sea
but it is grounded.
Beyond it, marking the line of horizon,
a ship heading for Morocco.

And we go too.
Our bodies scented for love,
an exploration of the familiar
in the swirling tents of Bedouins:
tight-stretched hide, thumping,
clap of hands to oiled thighs,
touching the fire, then flying;
circles of small brass bells
on arms and legs,
ashen faces leaping at the liquid rushing wail,
eyes rolling,
tongues tapping time;
the droning melody, haunted whine,
hatching in dry air
dancing girls with golden feathers.

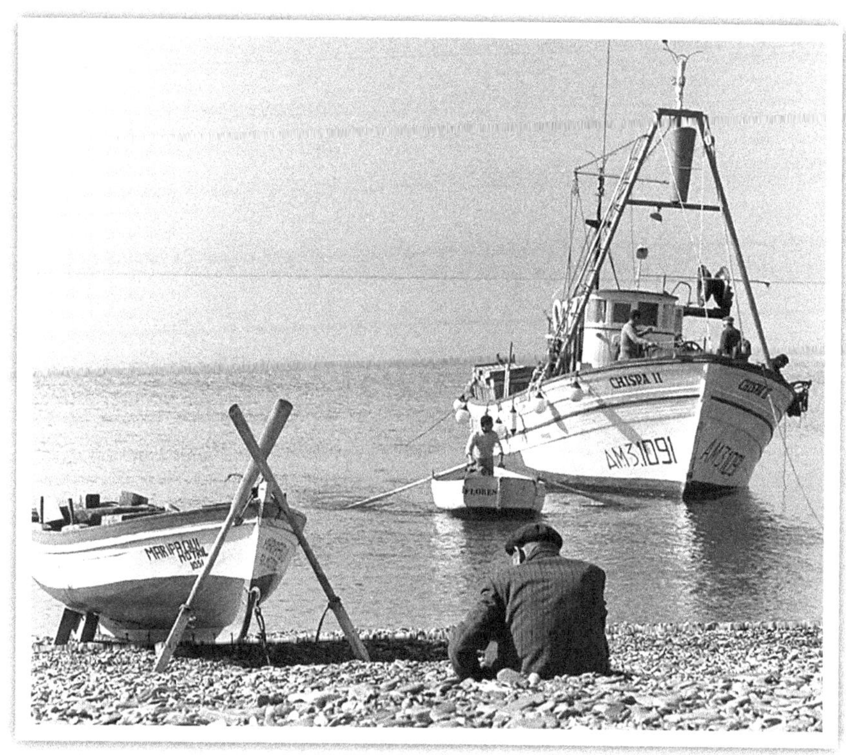

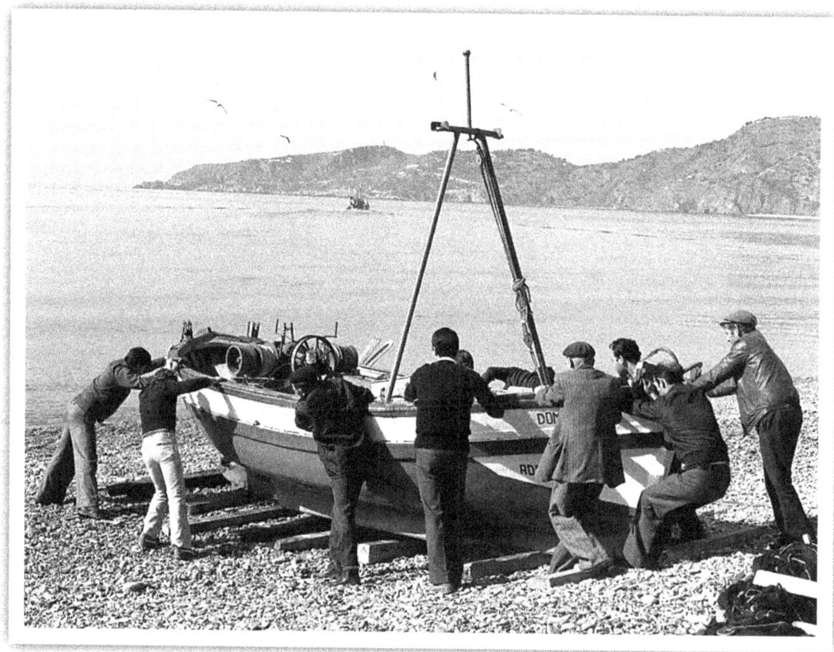

All photos in this chapter were taken in Almuñecar.

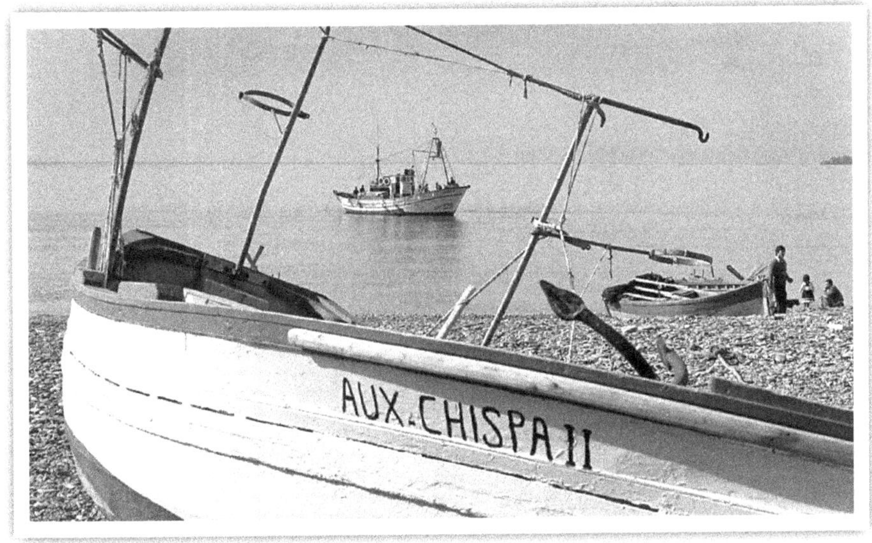
AUX. CHISPA II

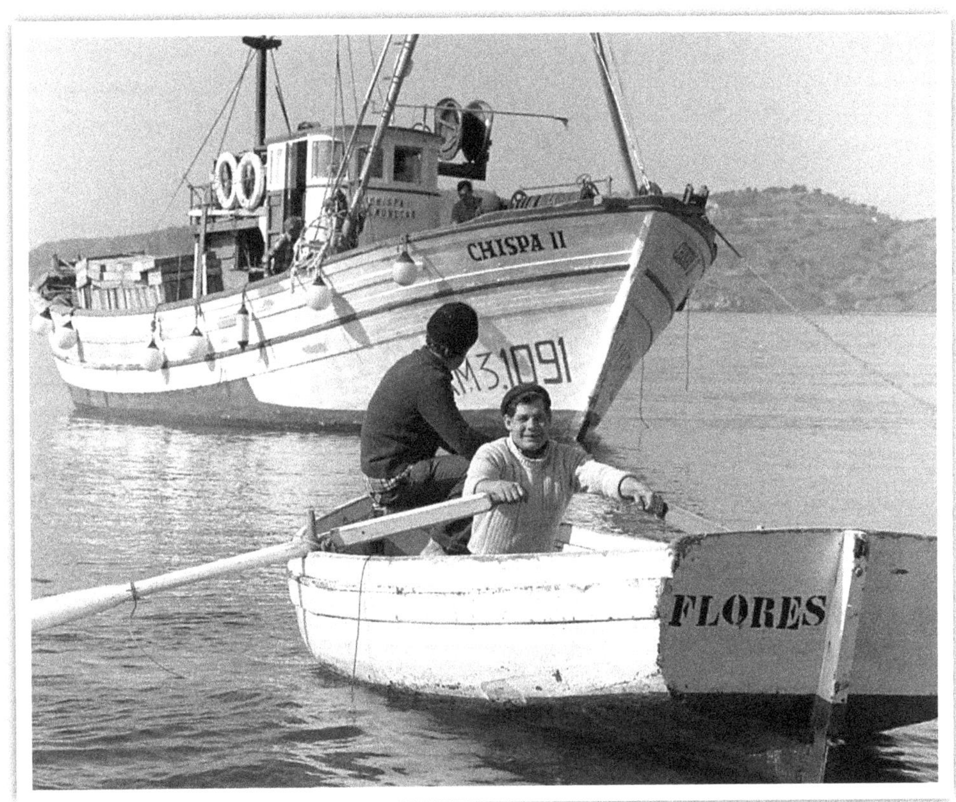
CHISPA II
FLORES

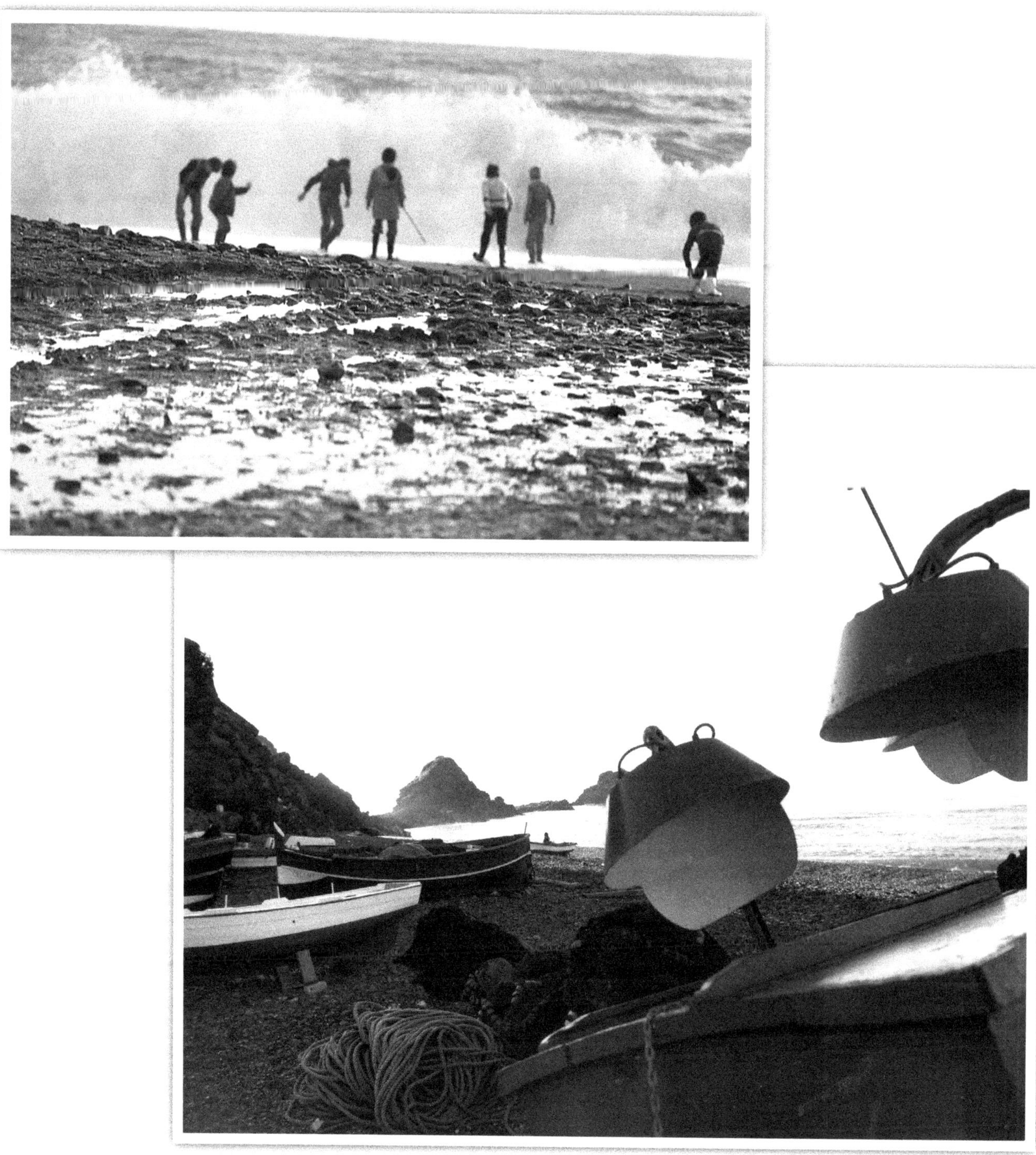

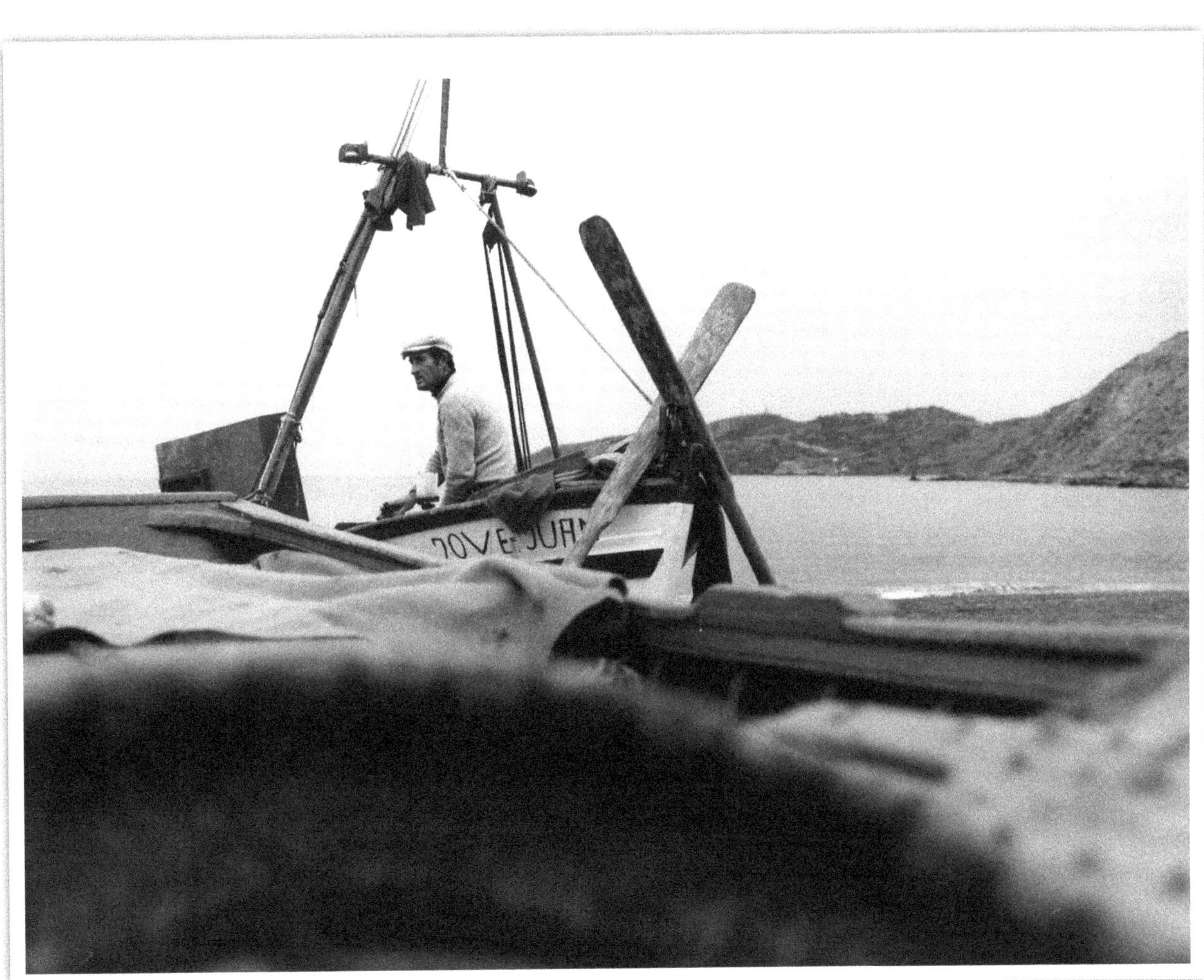
JOVE

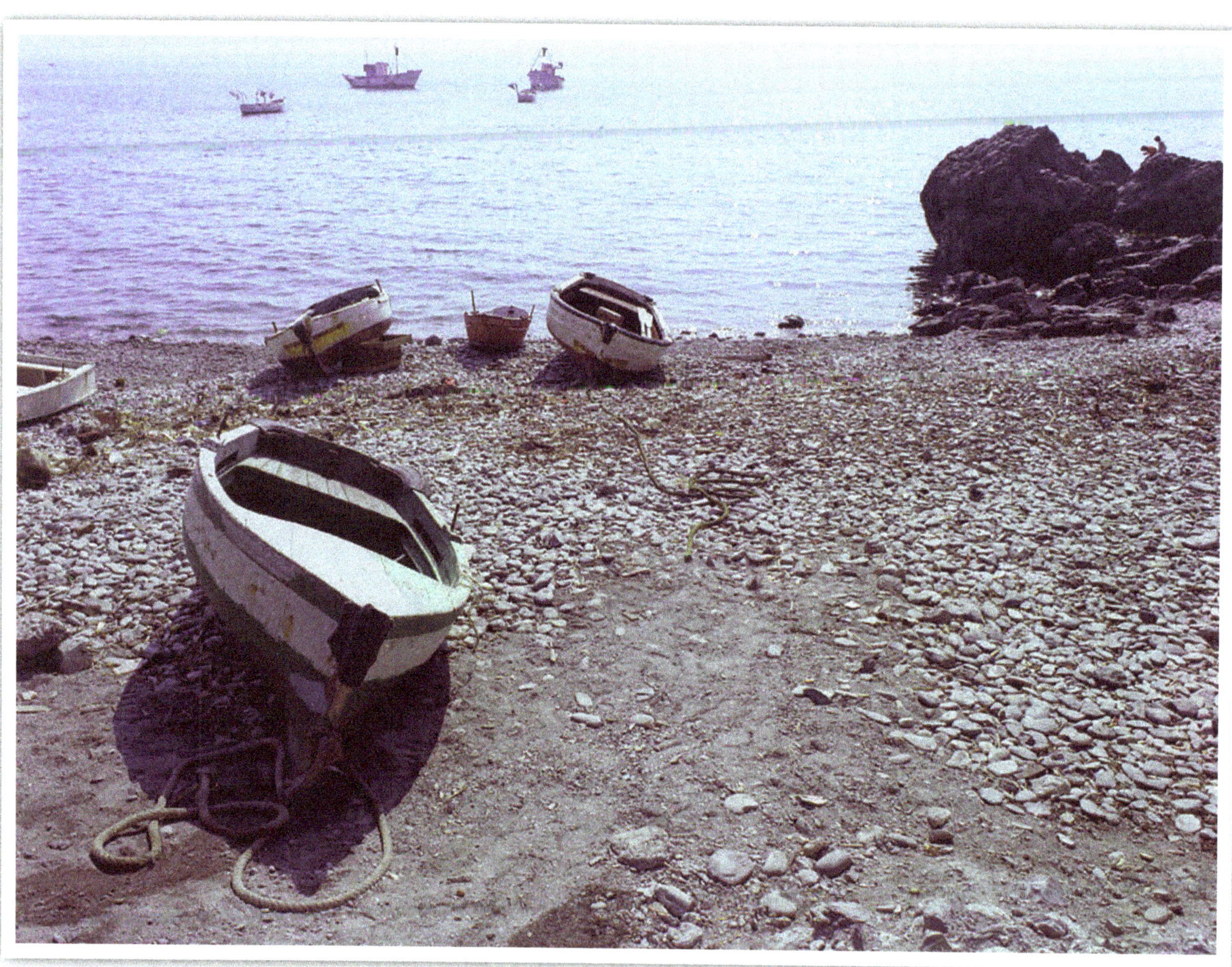

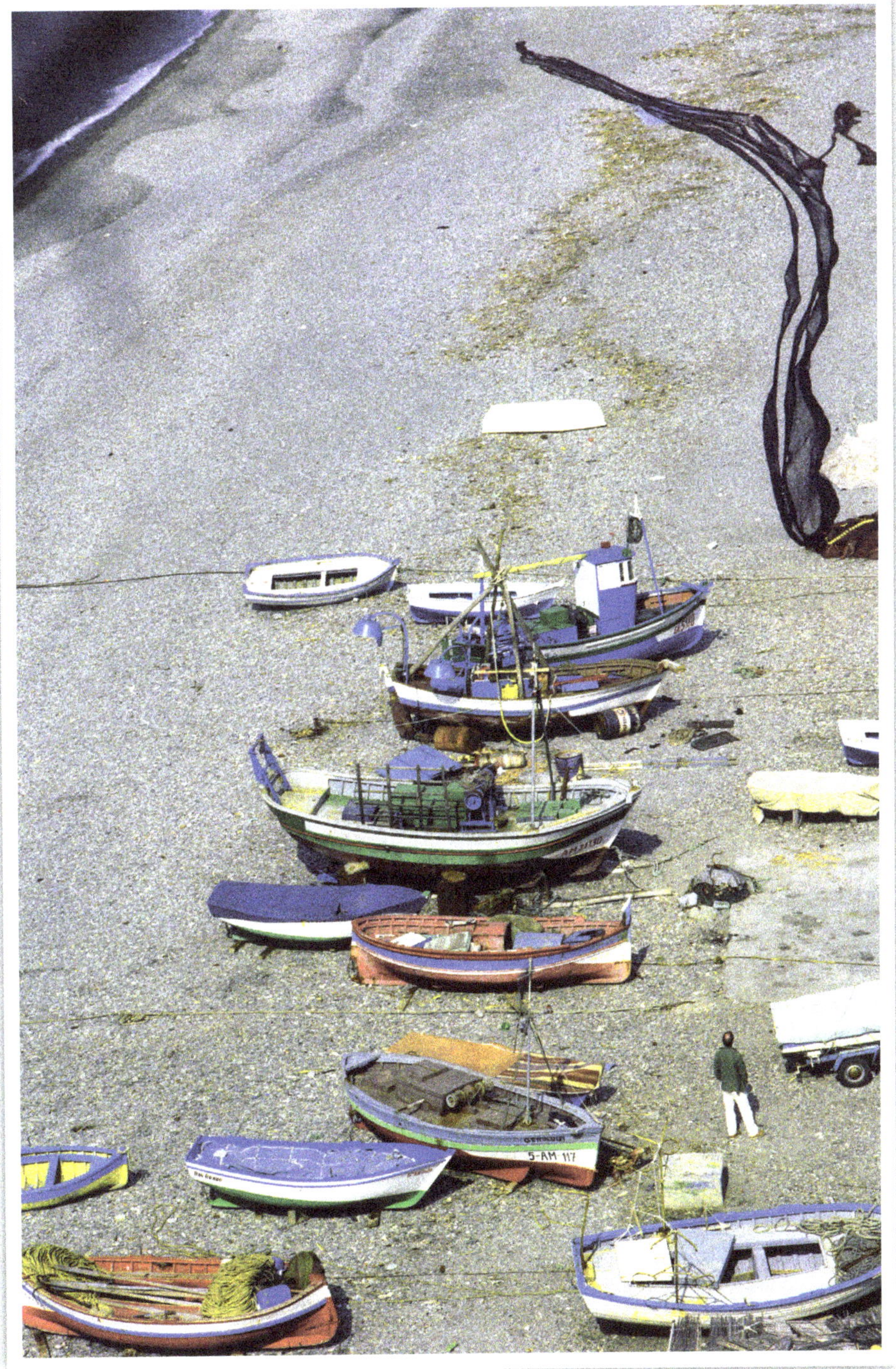
5-AM 117

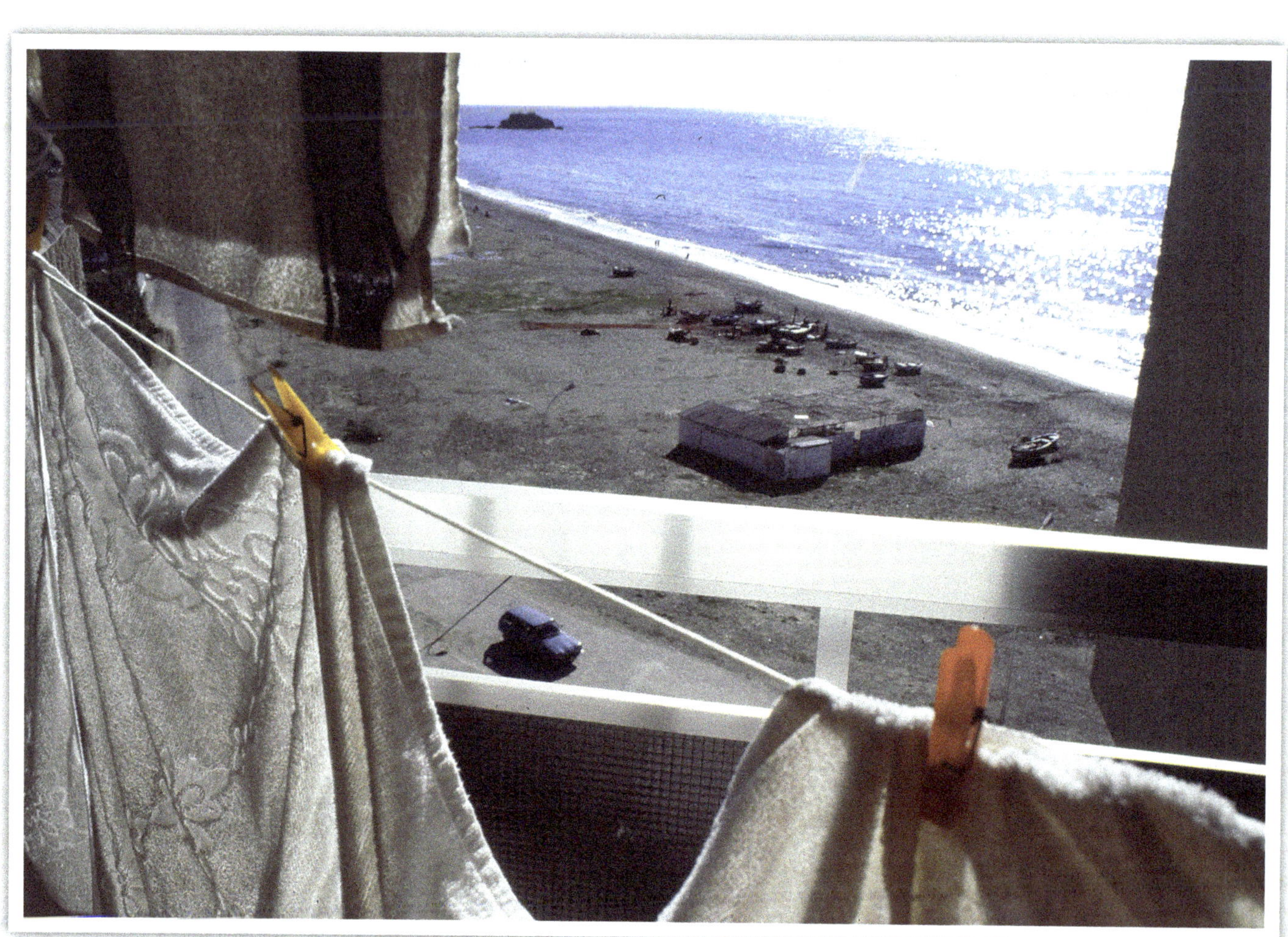

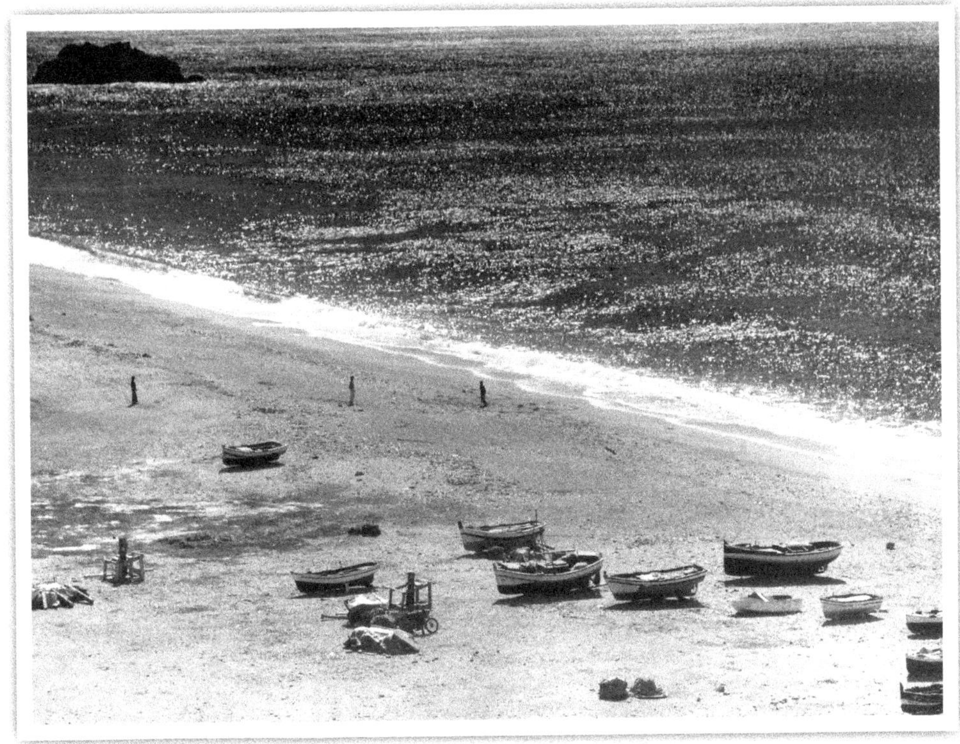

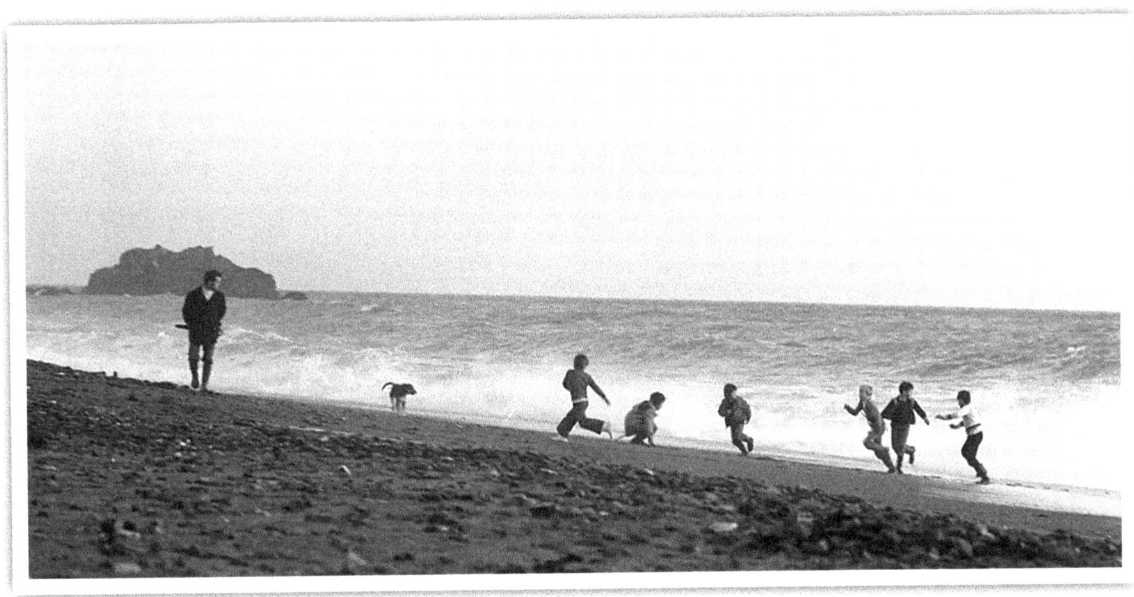

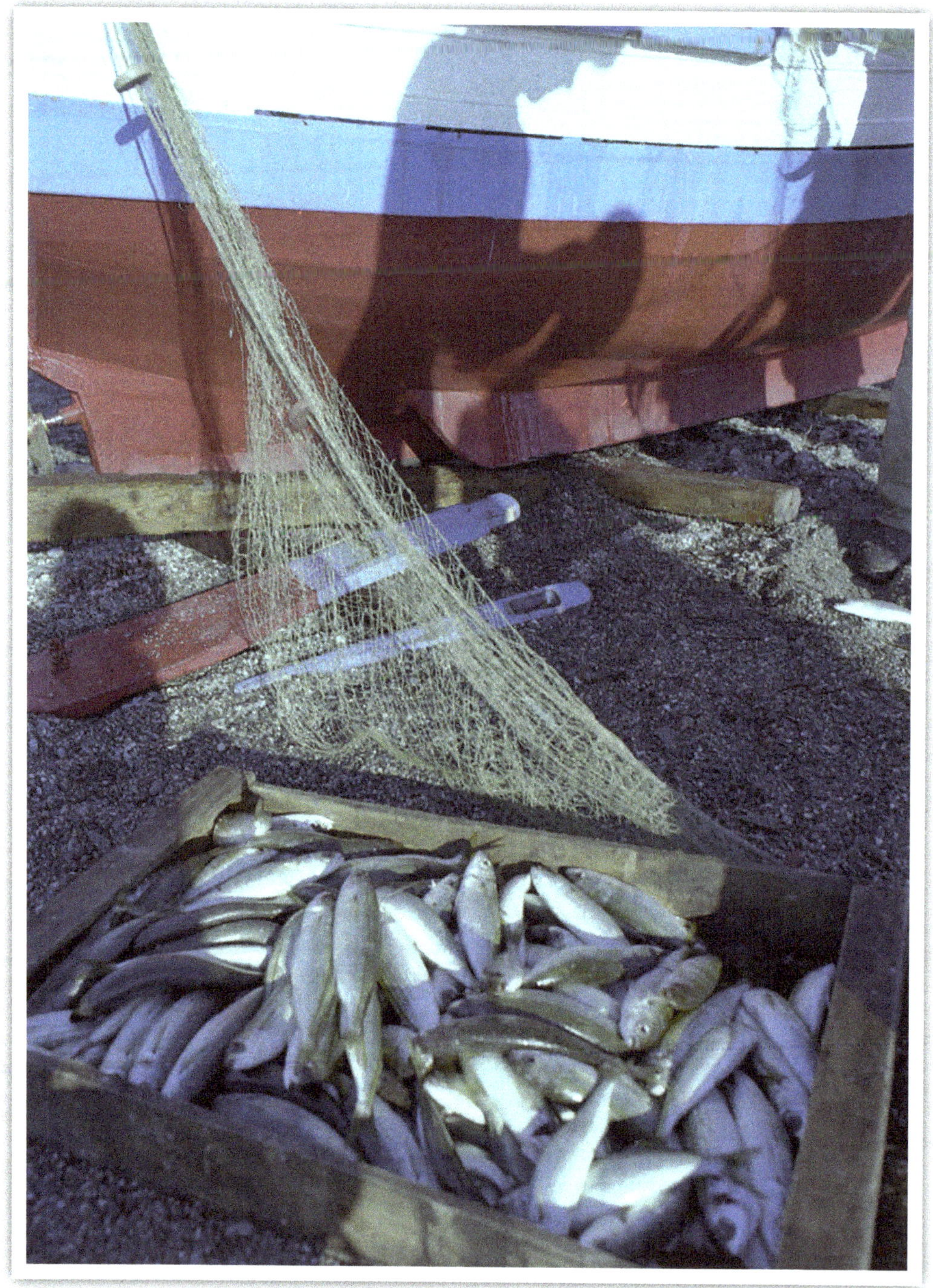

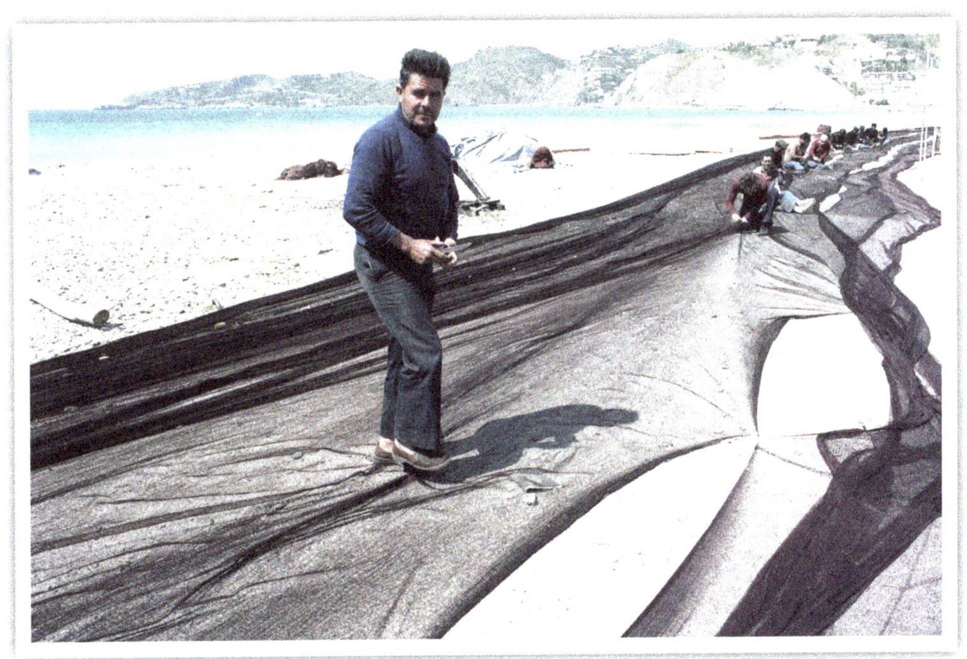

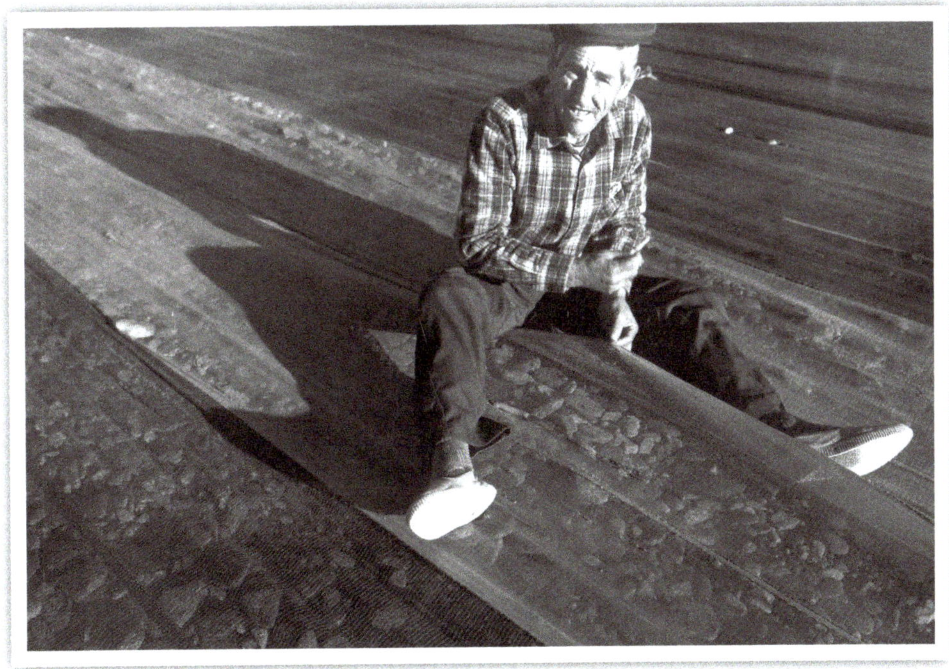

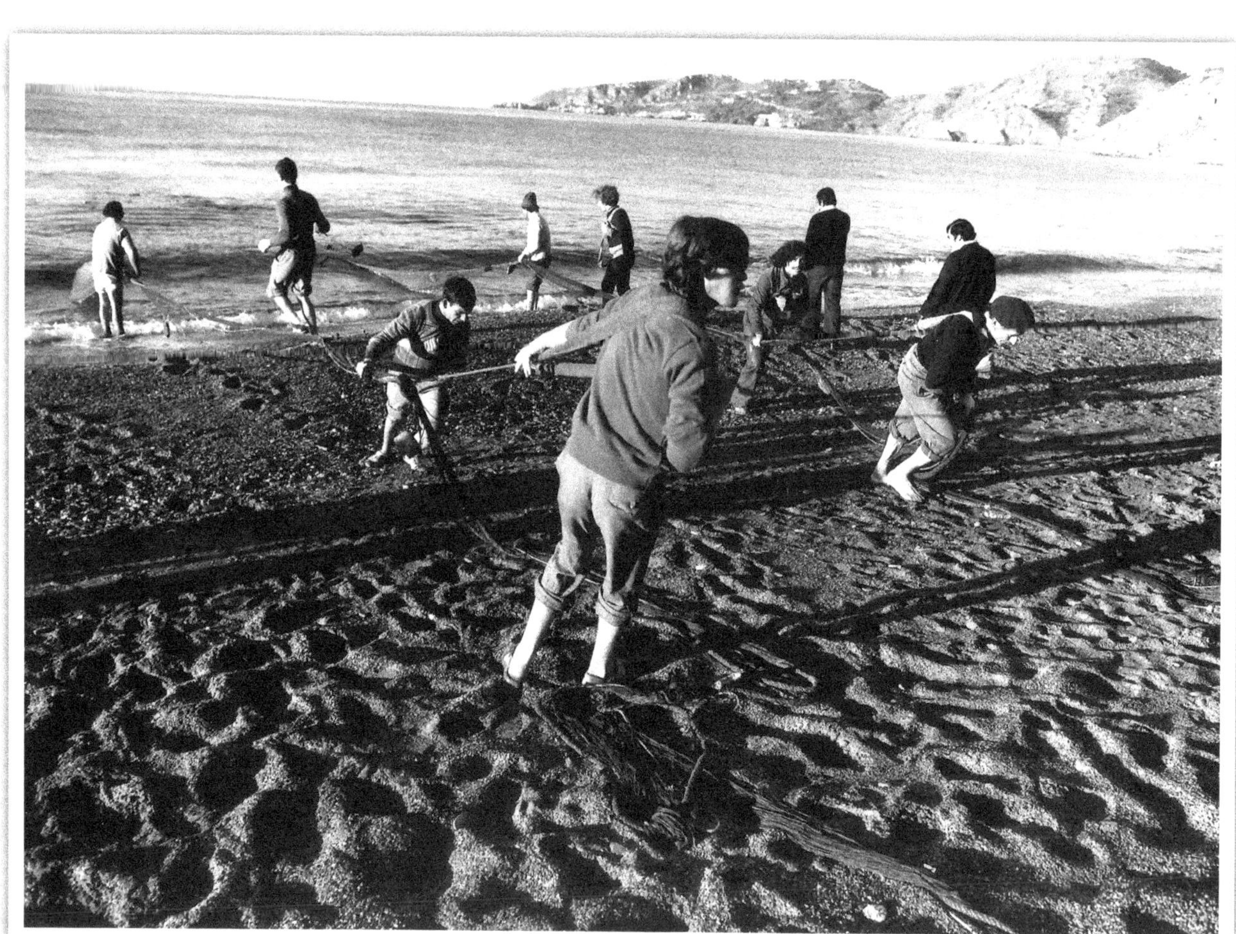

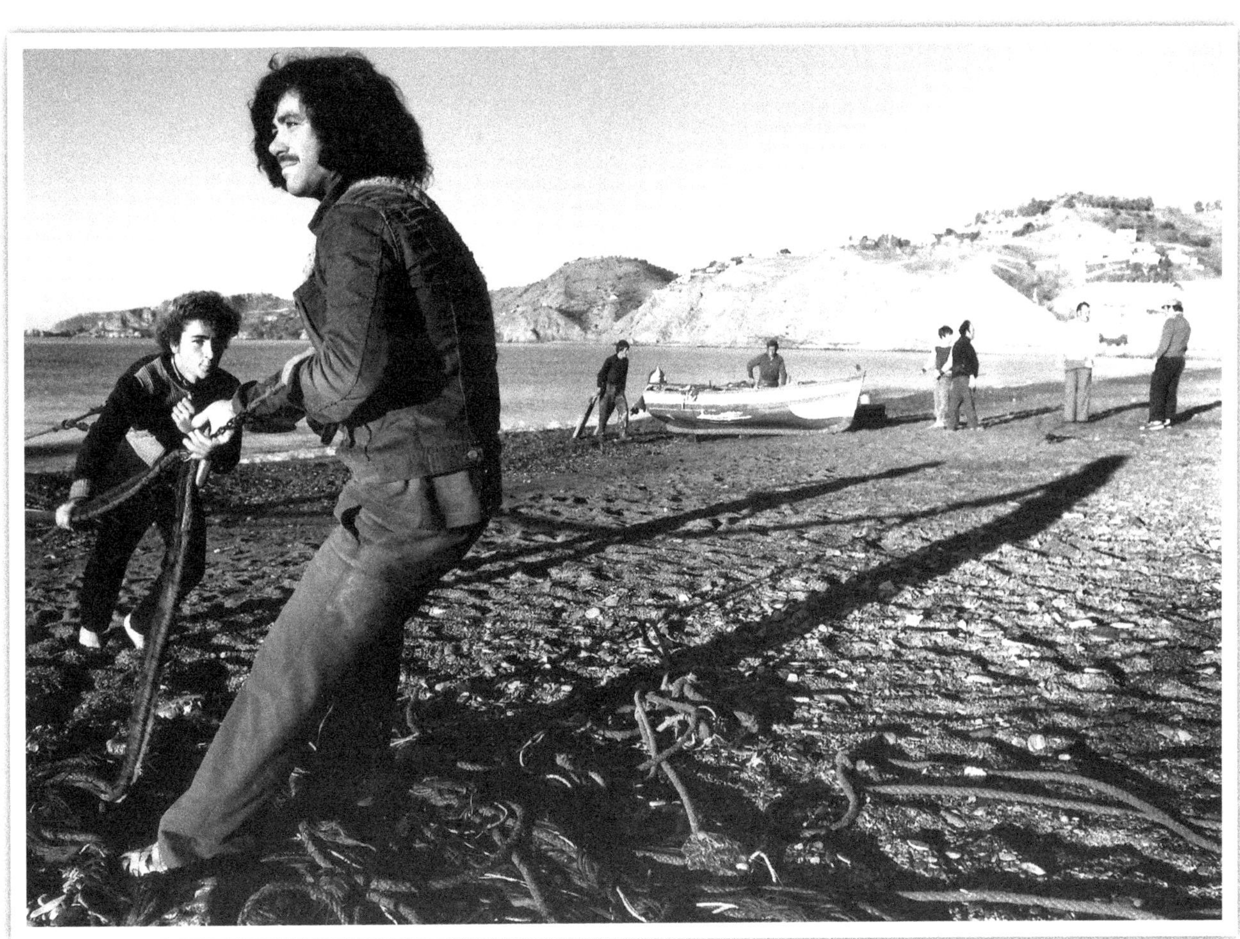

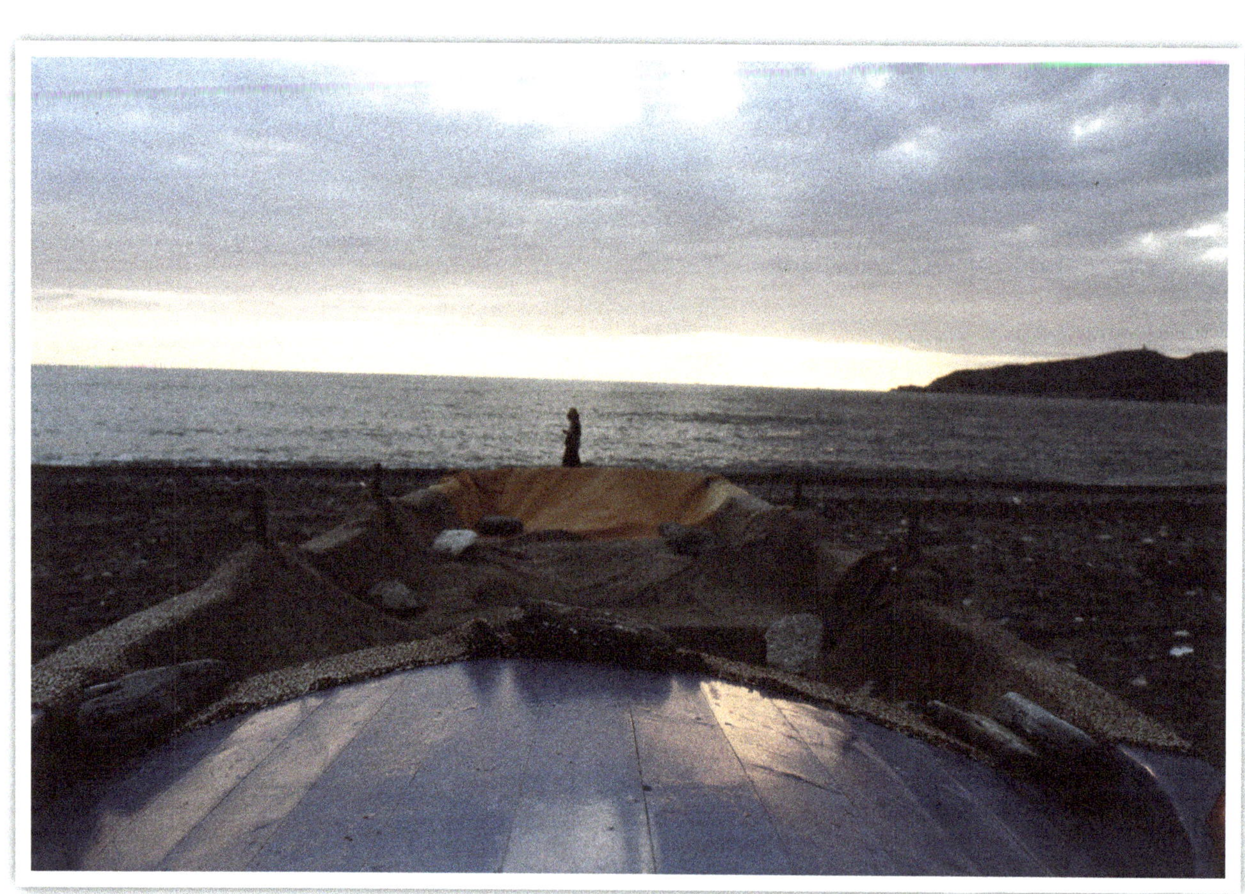

Village of Dreams

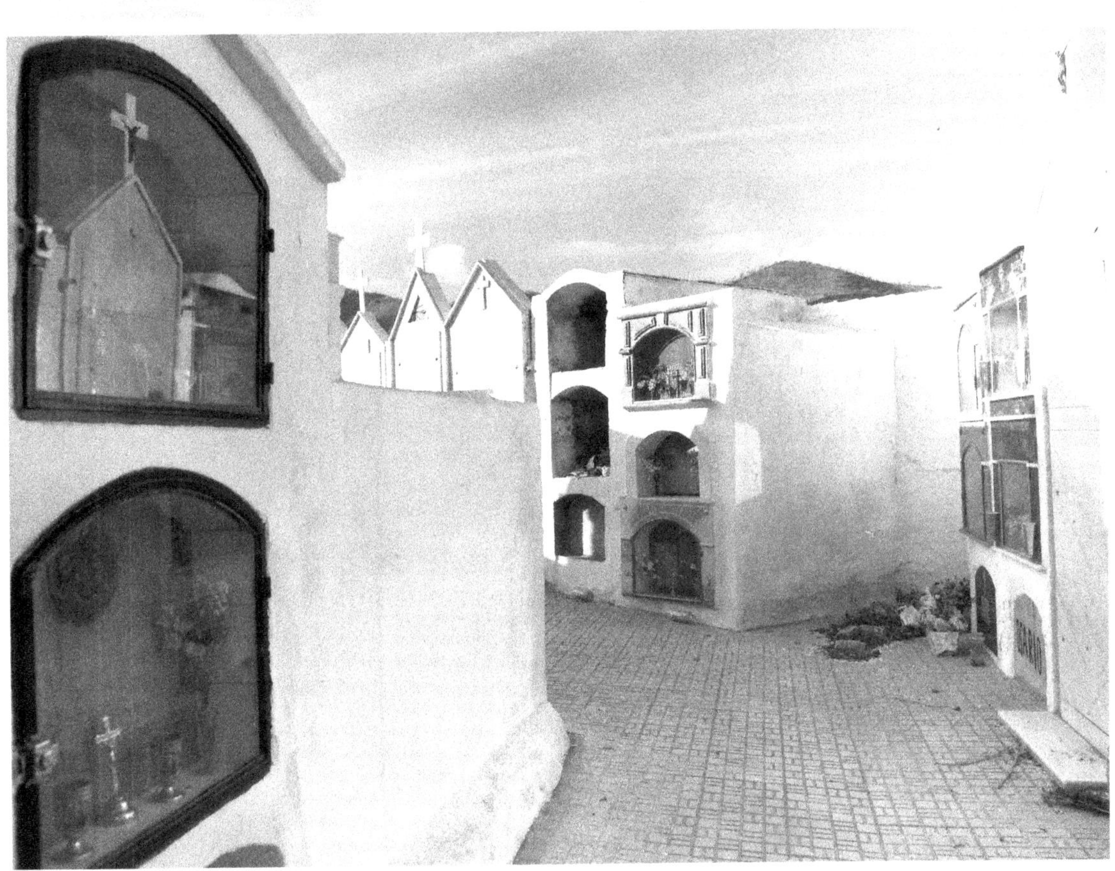

Village of Dreams

An old woman and I look out to sea
from the ramparts of the Moorish castle,
converted years ago to the village cemetery.
I wonder who built the tiny houses that hold the graves.
Who ditched the earth to mount a rock fortress,
afraid the body's blood feared water?

Village within a village, a *pueblo* of dreams and sleep:
the village cemetery perched on the highest hill
above the village of life and day.

In the small coastal towns of Andalusia,
cemeteries are Spanish villages in miniature,
clusters of whitewashed houses
stacked one on the other providing shelter and eternal peace.
White-washed apartments with bay windows,
or shops with glass fronts,
face narrow streets and reflect
mountains, clouds, trees, clusters of other grave fronts.
From the ramparts one sees a scattering of fishing boats,
dark flecks on the bright mirror of water.

She talks to me of fishing boats
and the routines of fishing people,
distracts me with the news of weather and sea storms
and sand blowing eternal from Africa.
Her crooked hand moves over the horizon
as if she's done this before, this visiting with strangers
on her visiting days.

But now I am alone again to see and photograph.
Workmen mend cobbles,
prop up an aging palm tree.
Women sweep paths with twig brooms,
talk loudly of children and
the high price of food.
Walls crumble while others are repaired:
a rusting bucket, a half-used bag of cement.
Cornered by the wind against the sides of graves,
fallen leaves chase in endless circles.

Another old woman wanders down a path.
At first I see only her shadow
so small and stooped and hard edged against the white wall.
She stops among the squat weeds, the daisies and clover,
rattles at a glass door,
fiddles with a key, crosses herself and prays.

When she leaves I go to the same grave
to see my face mirrored ghostlike and transparent
over mementos encased behind glass,
artifacts of the dead:
flowers, real and plastic,
a statue of the Virgin, Christ on the cross,
a photograph of a man with autographed greetings
from his family.

Bared to the sun
his face has faded to agelessness.
The edges of the paper have turned a mottled amber.
He looks out now at a prism of whitewashed angles in glass,
reflections of names and dates incised in stone,
his neighbors in faith:
beginnings and endings within the infinite questions
of the ruins.

And behind this glass door
he is dreaming of childhood friends
and one long journey when he rode against the night wind
on a cart with three young brothers.

He travels again in his dreams,
leaps over the low wall
away from the sounds of tumbling rock and
the heavy steps of his visitors.
They wrinkle and sag in their mourning black
as he grows young
in this village of dreams,
young as the crying sea or
the mountains waking to the slap of cold spring rains.

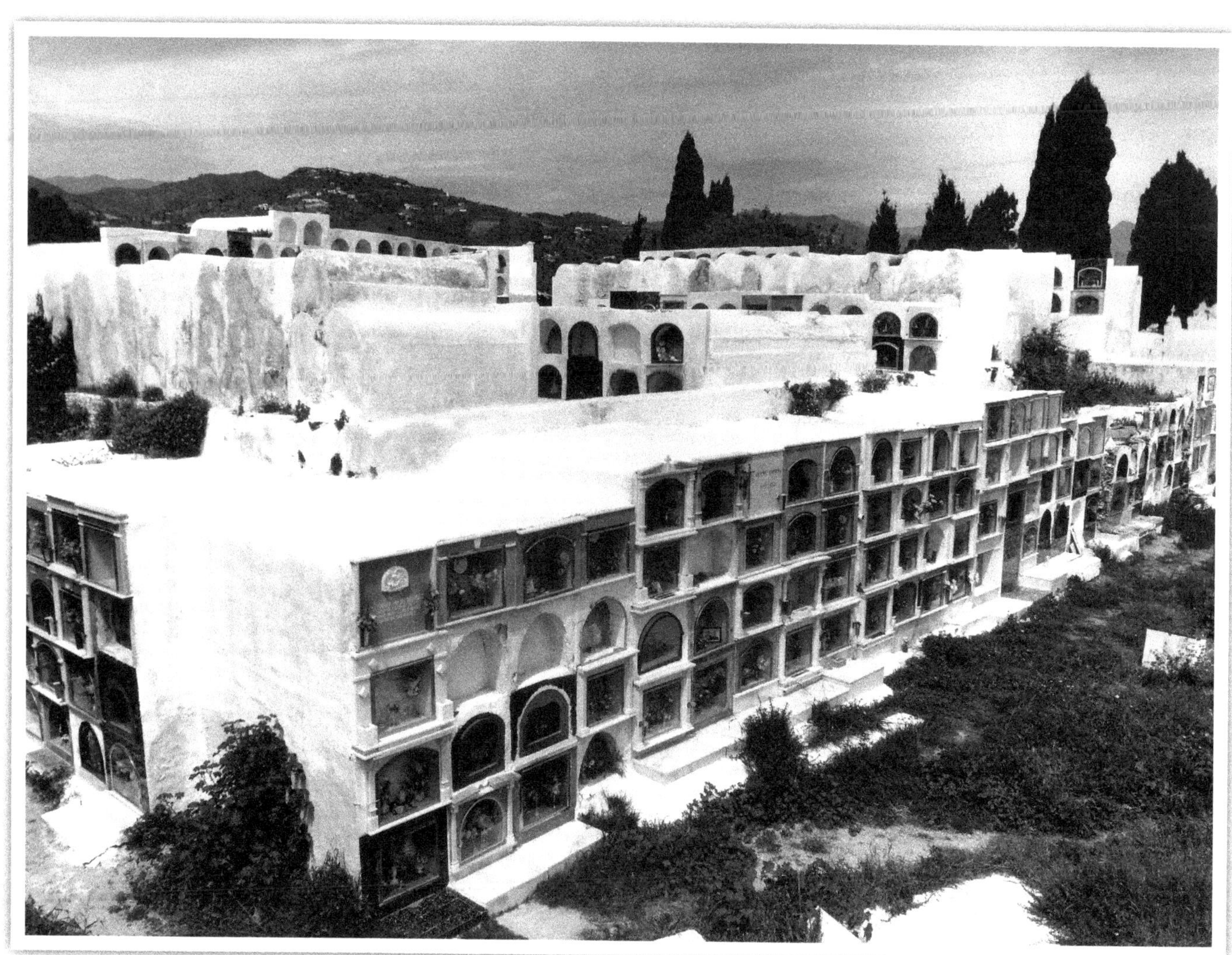

All photos in this chapter were taken in cemeteries in Almuñecar and Salobreña.

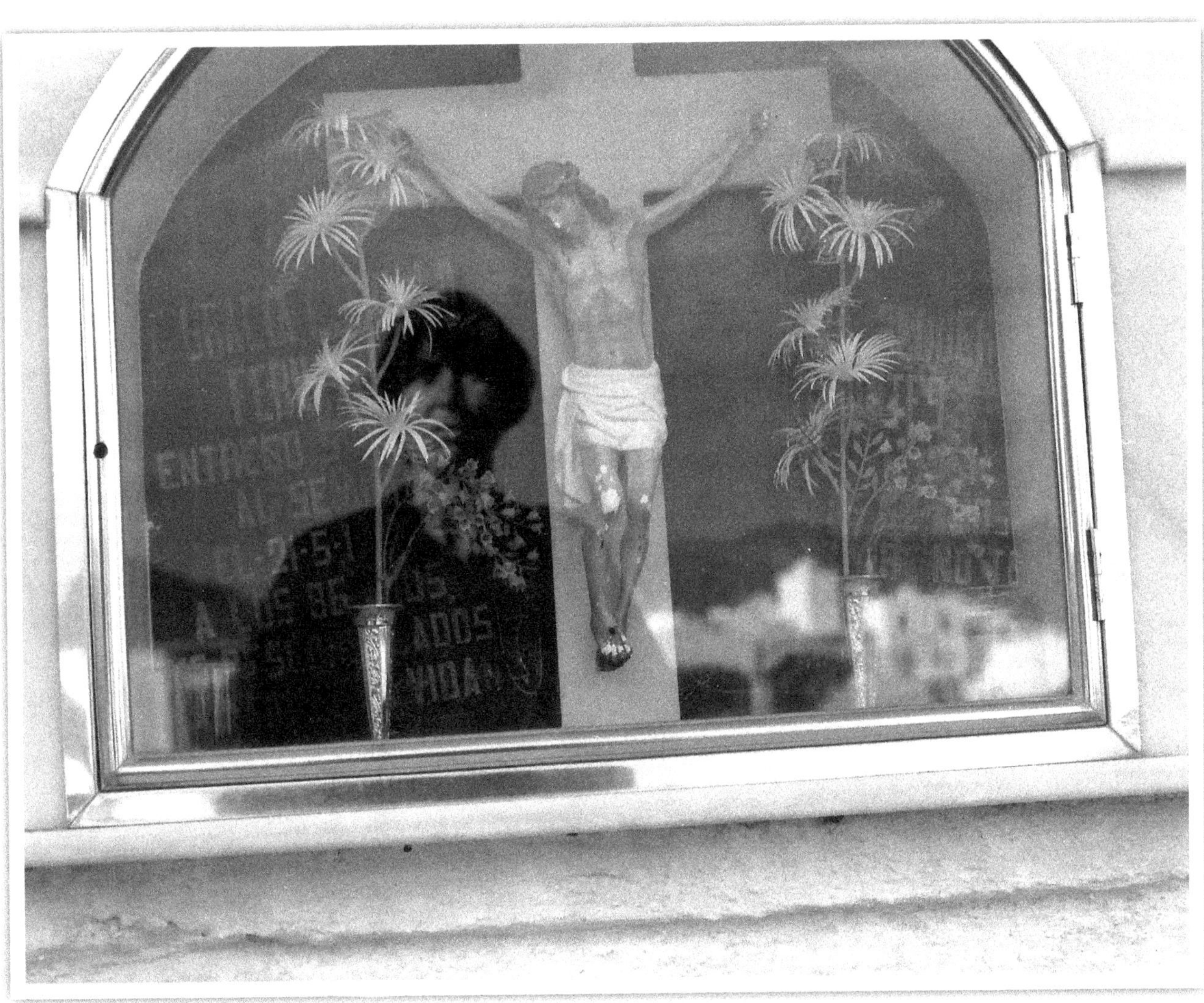

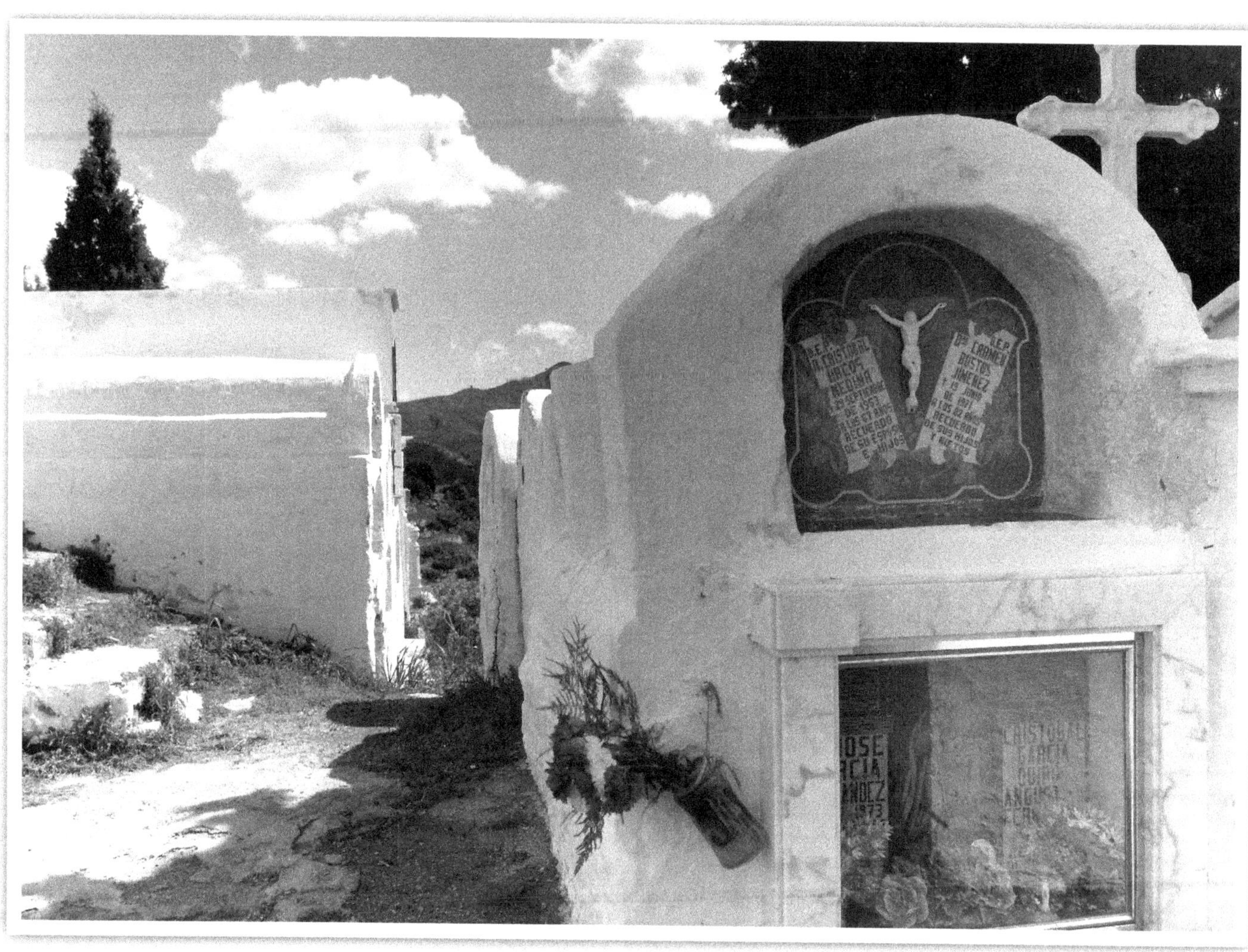

D. CRISTOBAL
Dª CARMEN
BUSTOS
JIMENEZ
RECUERDO
DE SUS HIJOS

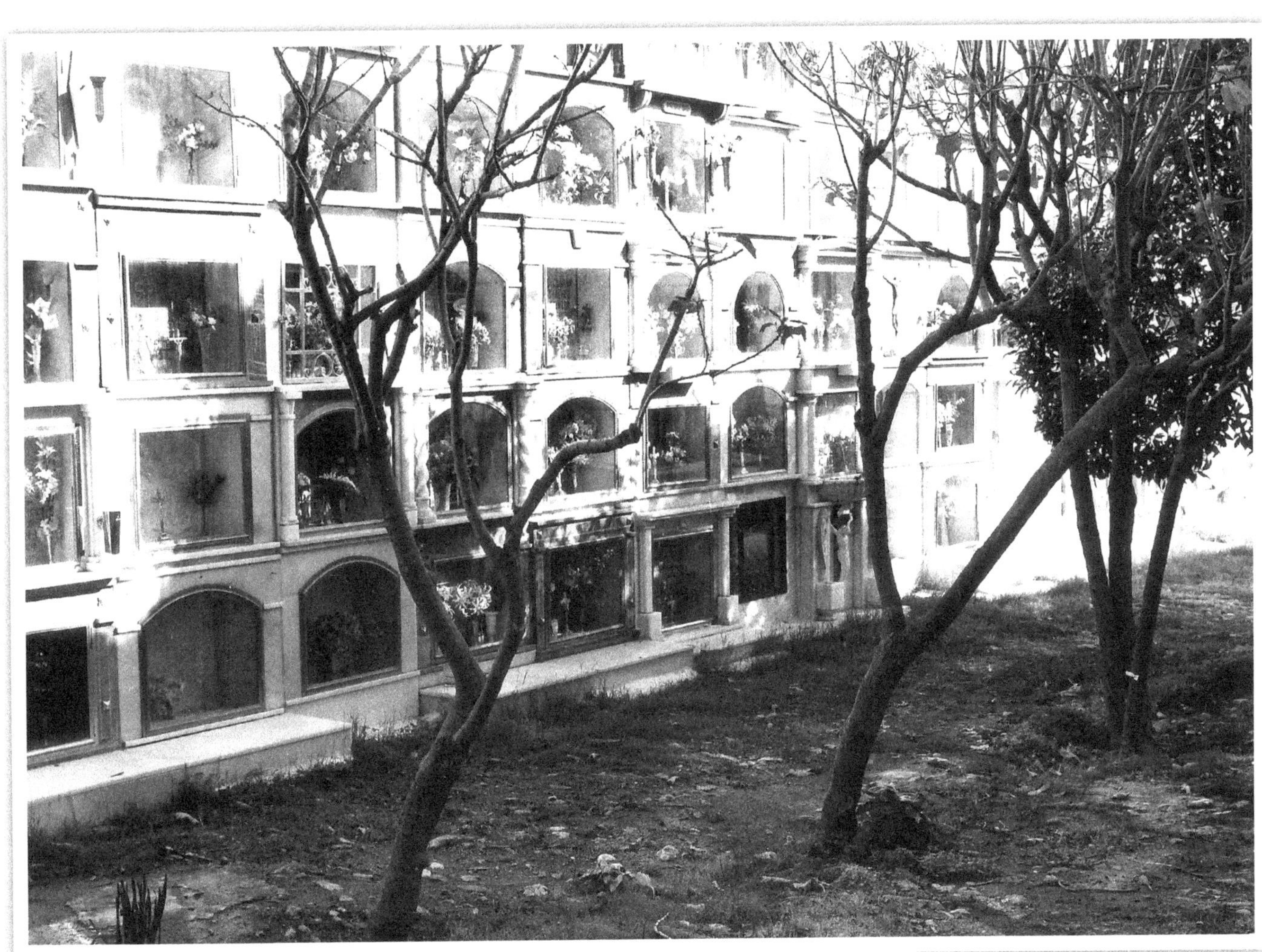

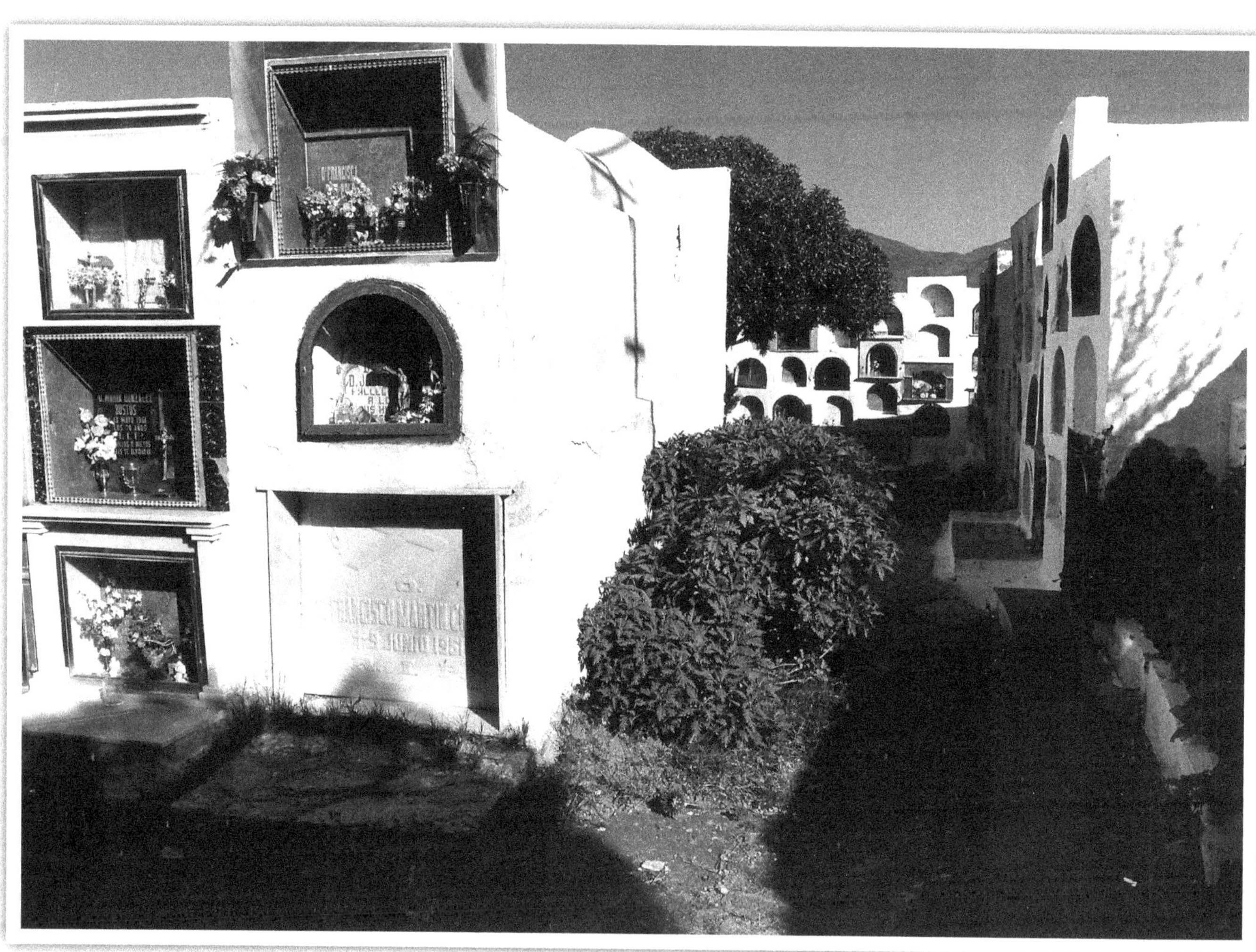

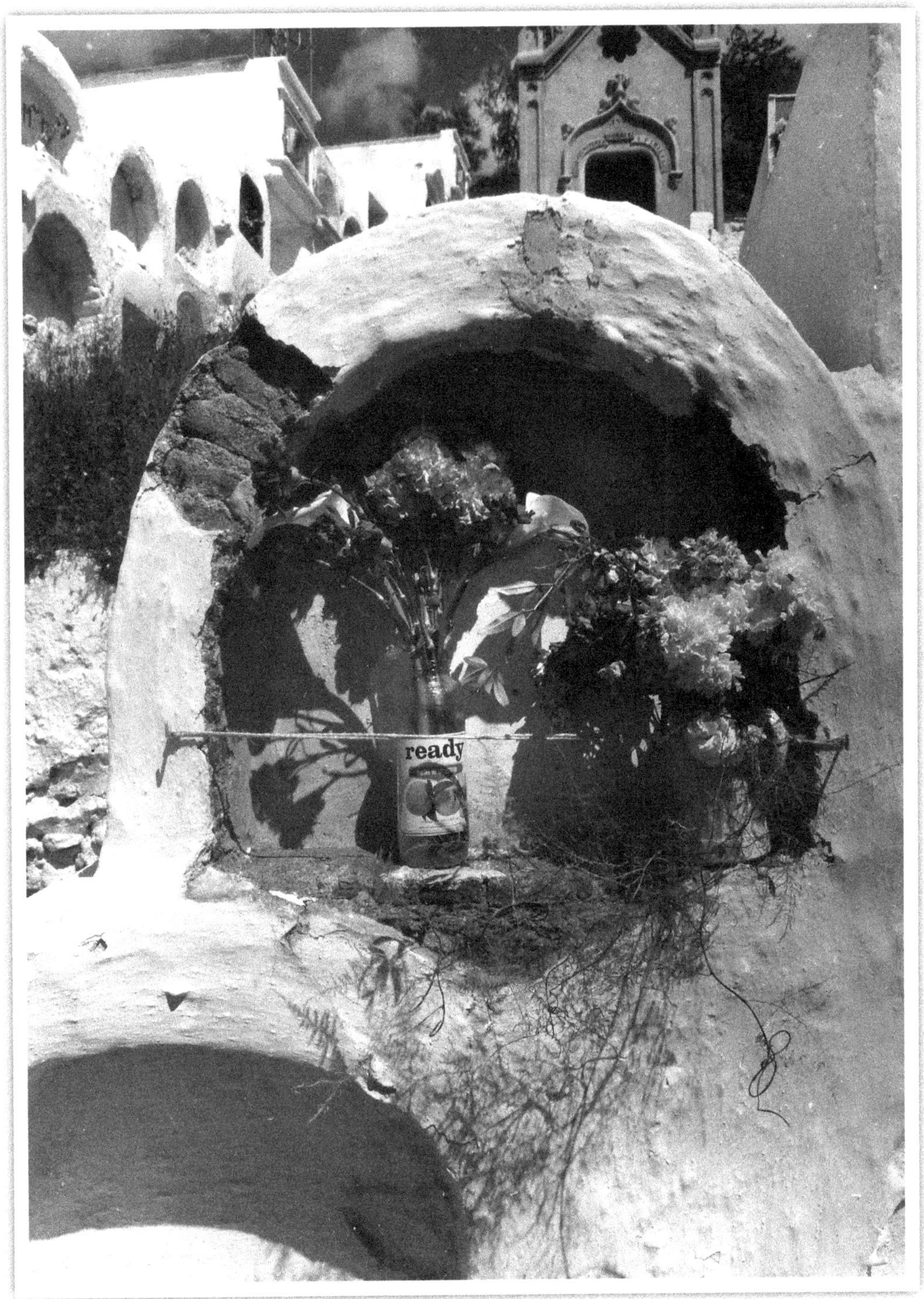
ready

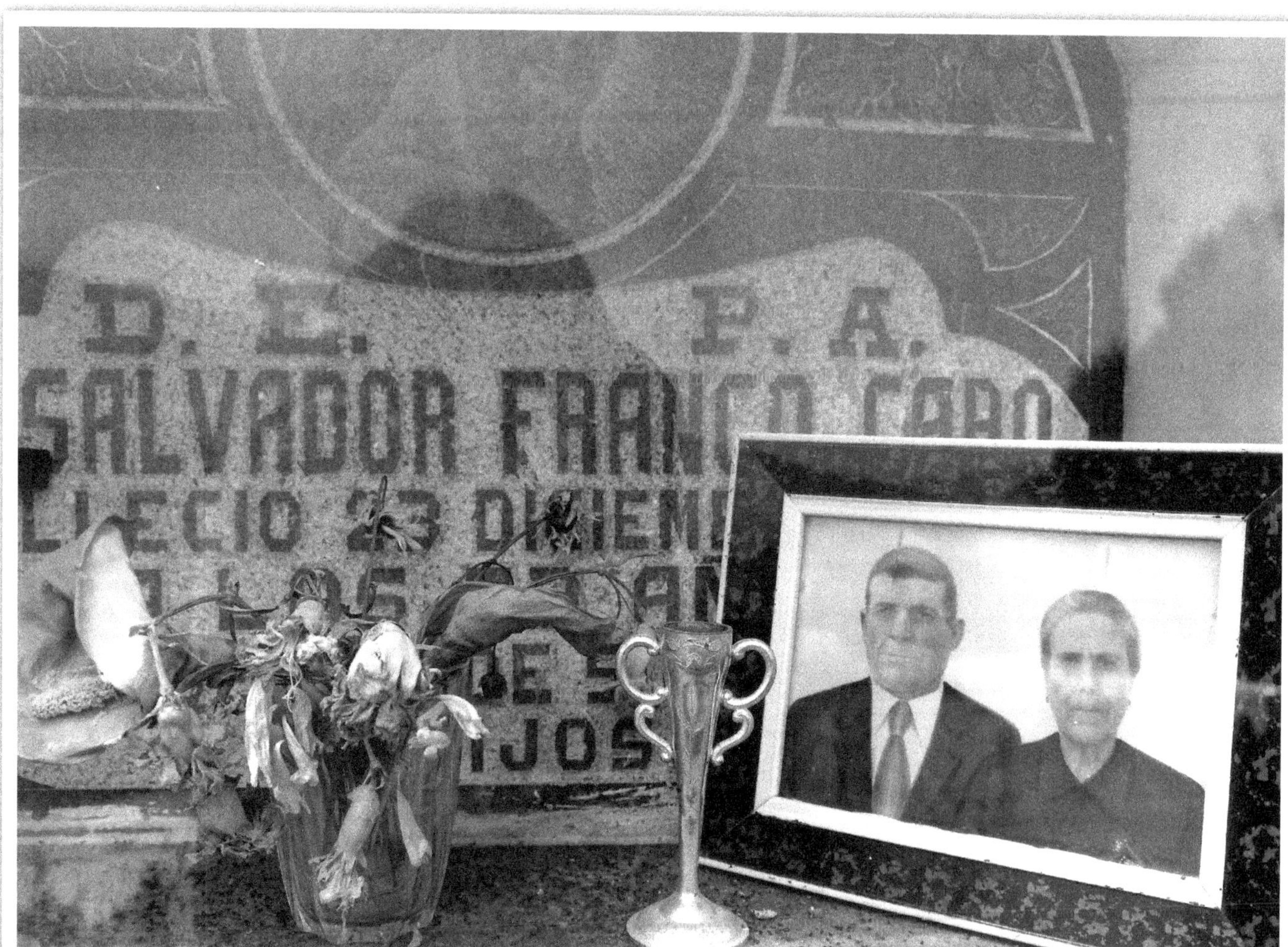
D. E. P. A.
SALVADOR FRANCO CARO

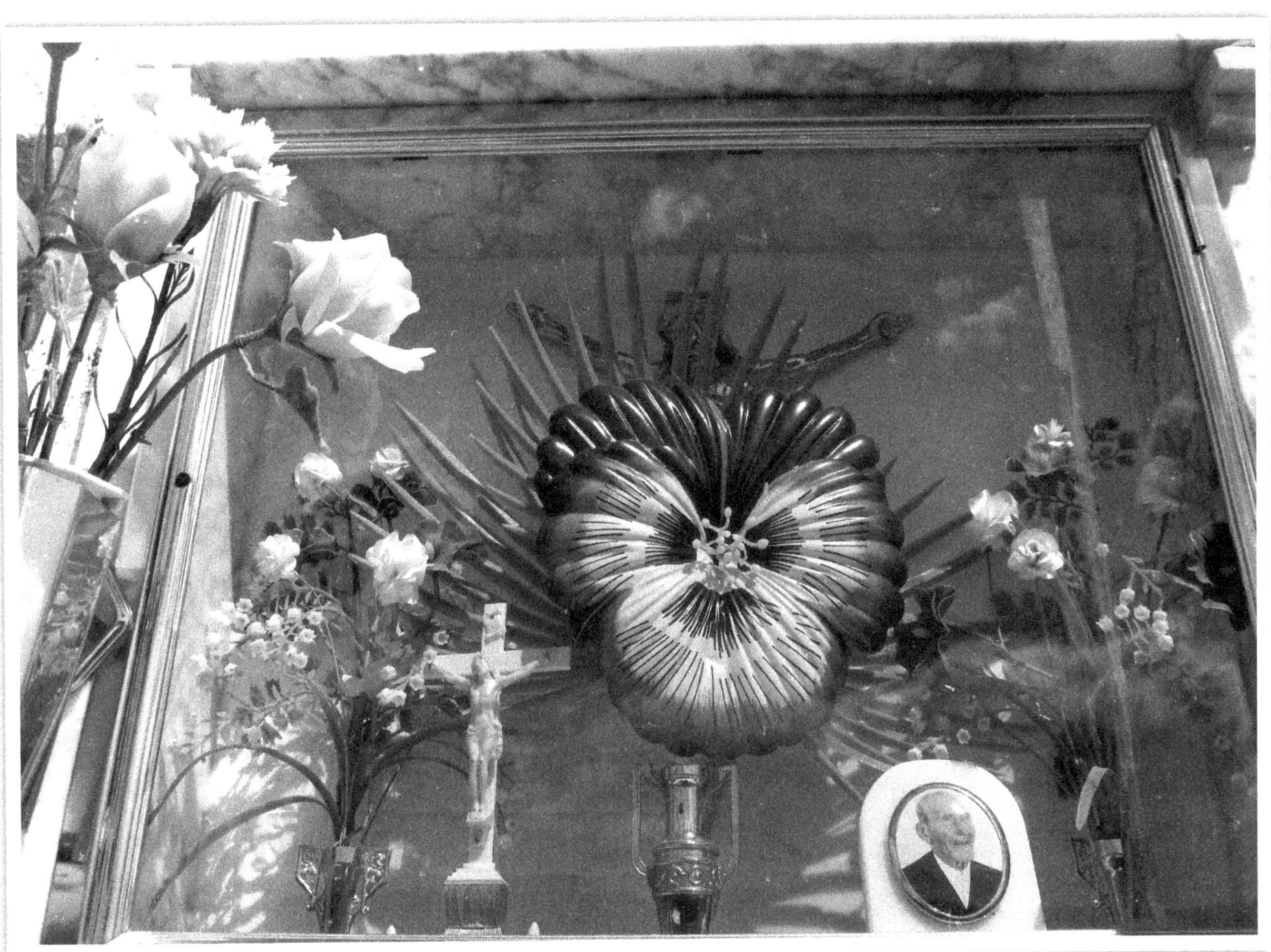

Epilogue

I took this photo nearly 40 years ago in Almuñecar. It was one of several political posters that urged people to vote in our little beach town. It was a time of change. *Generalissimo* Franco had died in 1975 and within a few years Spain was turning to democracy. Although King Juan Carlos was Franco's designated successor, tutored and tailored to maintain the principles of Franco's National Movement, the 1978 constitution made Spain a parliamentary democracy. In 1981 the monarch ignored Franco's supporters and rejected a military coup, once again upholding Spain's democracy.

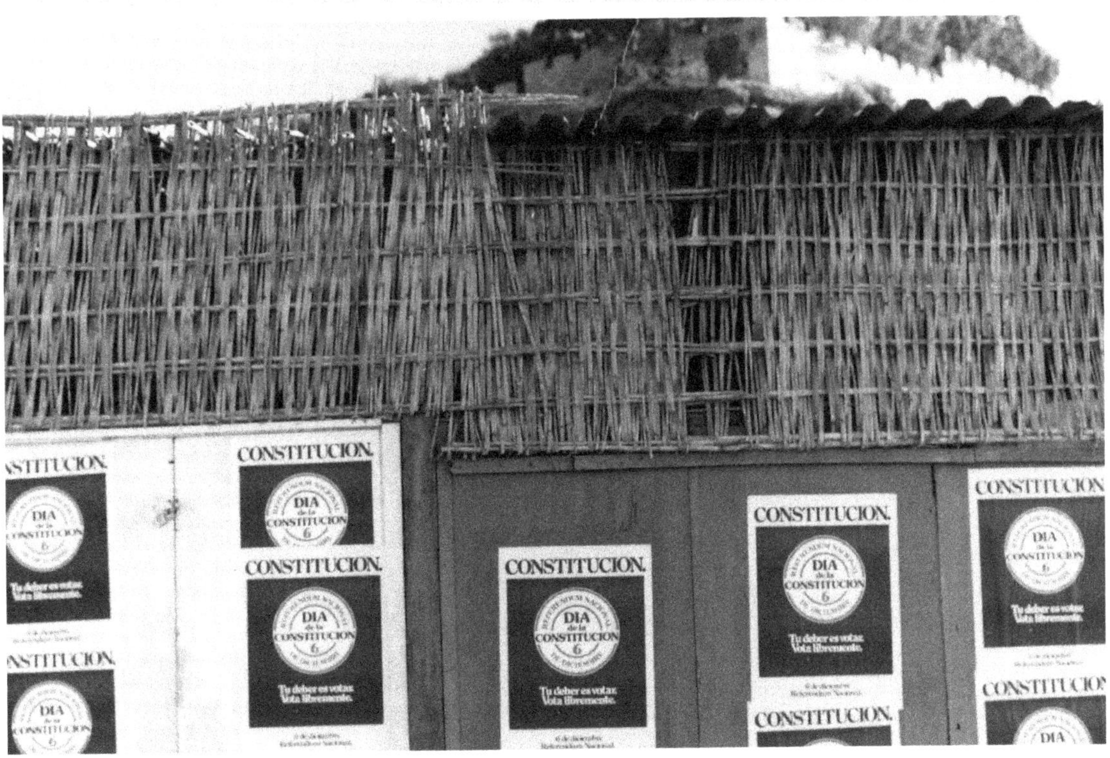

Now, as this book goes to press, Spain is facing its most serious constitutional crisis in nearly 40 years. Catalan independence threatens the social fabric of modern Spain and is illegal, according to the Spanish court. Those who support independence, or simply the right to vote for self-determination, raise the specter of Franco and his repressive regime, and the horrors of the Spanish Civil War. There are deep divides within the region, and even within families, as brother and sister stand on different sides of the issue. As an outsider, and a non-historian outsider, I miss the nuances of Spanish politics and have relied on BBC News and the perspective of my Spanish friends for my information. Is Spain in crisis or in transition? Can autonomous regions stretch their political will within the boundaries set by nationhood?

This book is part memoir, part chapbook of poems, part photographic celebration of the Spain I first encountered nearly 40 years ago. It was the Spain of mountain villages, small coastal towns, and a waning rural lifestyle. As I was preparing these photographs and poems for publication, I was surprised at how much I had forgotten. The more boxes of negatives and prints I opened and dusted off, the more I found to enjoy. Many years ago I fell in love with the country's beautiful landscape and its generous people. As I think now about my first encounters with Spain—the glorious hikes in the *Picos de Europa* and Pyrenees, the more I want to go back and put my feet on those same trails if only for a few steps.

I had returned to Almuñecar twice since my winter there in the late 1970s. The first time, in 2000, I noticed some changes. The town looked more tidy and there were urban design and infrastructure improvements along the *malecón*, probably a benefit of Spain's membership in the European Union. In February of this year I hardly recognized the Almuñecar I had loved. New roads, hotels, offices, restaurants—an explosion of new development to serve ex-pats and tourists, formed a tight ring around the old town. Trapped in traffic, I could hardly see the church tower or find my way to the *malecón*. The economy may be better now and the grandchildren of the fishermen I had photographed may have better schools and a brighter future. But those schools are likely elsewhere. I saw no fishing boats on my beach and, in what had been a pristine cove, I saw an upscale marina. As with so much of the Spain I knew, my small fishing village, my small town with an historic heart, exists only in my memory.

San Carlos, Sonora, Mexico, March 2018

Acknowledgments

I don't believe in angels or demons but I do believe in miracles, blind luck, and twists of fate. The first chapter in this book looks back at some happy circumstances that led to my on-going love affair with Spain. It is an extended thank you and memorial to Jack and Barbara Masters, and to my late husband, Don Dubois. Without them I may not have visited Spain 40 years ago nor had the opportunity to return again and again.

Love, luck, and laughter inspired the vows Charlie Bloomer and I exchanged nearly ten years ago. I thank him for his love and support, and our good friend, Caroline Durand, for always being willing to share in our Spanish adventures.

I thank my Spanish friends for their hospitality and generosity of spirit: Tomás Recio, Isabel Miranda, Carlos Andradas, Lina Arias, and Cristina Nuñez de Villavicencio.

I thank the youngsters I photographed so many years ago who are now in late middle-age, and *los ancianos,* the old women in black, and the goatherds and fishermen, who are long gone. Finally, I thank my readers. My photographs and poems live in a distant time but because of you they have come alive.

About the Author/Photographer

Barbara Strelke is a poet, photographer, and painter who divides her time between San Carlos, Sonora, Mexico, and Tucson, Arizona. She shares her life and future travels in Spain with Charlie Bloomer. In her previous careers she taught English and ethnic literature at the University of New Mexico, history of landscape architecture at the University of Arizona, and worked as a land use planner for city and county governments in Tucson. Near the end of her planning career, she opened a private consulting firm, which allowed her the time and freedom to revisit her love of painting. Visit her artist's website at www.barbarastrelke.com.

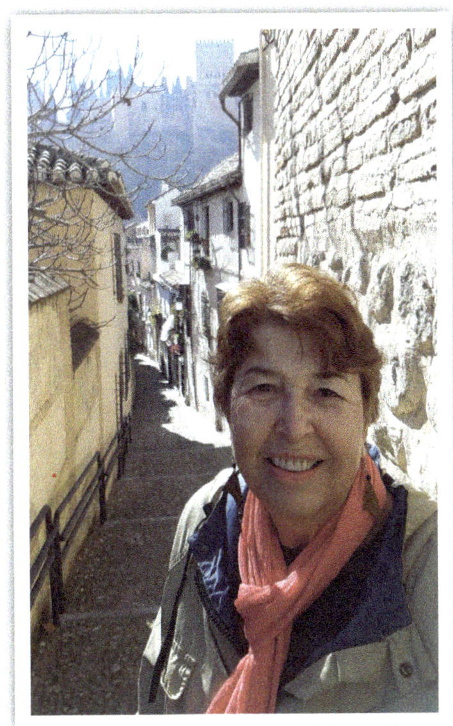

Granada, 2018 (photo by Charlie Bloomer)

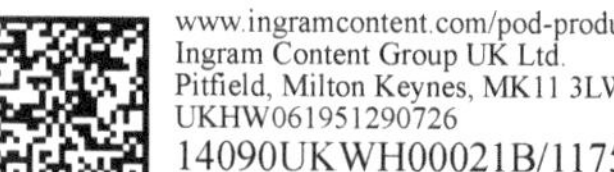
www.ingramcontent.com/pod-product-compliance
Ingram Content Group UK Ltd.
Pitfield, Milton Keynes, MK11 3LW, UK
UKHW061951290726
14090UKWH00021B/1175

9 780692 098639